ALL-AMERICAN DOGS

A HISTORY OF PRESIDENTIAL PETS FROM EVERY ERA

DEY ST.

An Imprint of WILLIAM MORROW

ALL-AMERICAN DOGS

ANDREW HAGER

HarperCollins books may be purchased for educational, business, or sales promotional use.
For information, please email the Special Markets Department at SPsales@harpercollins.com.

FIRST EDITION

Designed by Renata De Oliveira

Library of Congress Cataloging-in-Publication Data has been applied for.

ISBN 978-0-06-315827-6

22 23 24 25 26   LSC   10 9 8 7 6 5 4 3 2 1

FOR KRISTY,

even though she's a cat person

CONTENTS

INTRODUCTION

You've seen the news footage: A president exits his helicopter on the White House lawn. Waiting a few yards away is a staff member with a dog. The president waves to the assembled media, takes the leash from the staffer, and walks his dog into the White House. It's a ritual dating back decades, and one rarely questioned by the average American. Just the leader of the free world and his pet. Nothing to see here.

But once we follow human and dog through the doors to the Executive Mansion, there's a great deal to see.

Thirty-one of the forty-six United States presidents (and counting) have been dog owners. And from George Washington's hounds to Joe Biden's three German shepherds, presidential dogs have always captured the attention (and adoration) of Americans.

The political and cultural impact dogs have had on their respective owners in chief is often overlooked. There is a lot to unpack about the immeasurable effect they have had on these men (and sadly, to this point, it has been only men) and on Americans, and the ways in which the relationships with our canine companions have changed over the last two centuries.

This book is an exploration of the lives of presidential dogs throughout the nation's history. Its primary focus is on the animals themselves, in the context of their time and place, with the achievements or failures of their human masters left for other historians to analyze. Dogs have not been the only presidential pets—far from it. There have been cats, birds, snakes, tigers, silkworms, flying squirrels, a badger, a one-legged rooster, and a tobacco-chewing ram. Those animals, as interesting as they are, receive little attention in these pages. Many of these creatures are exotic and do not fit into the reality of the average citizen. Others, like the horses owned by every president prior to Woodrow Wilson, were not so much companions as they were transportation. Finally, the cats—America's second most popular pets—are less documented, perhaps because, unlike dogs, they cannot be walked or trained to sit quietly during a press conference. And while some of these other presidential pets make cameo appearances in this work, the dogs are front and center.

Of course, the human-canine relationship has evolved dramatically over the last 250 years. Our colonial-era forebears interacted very differently with their animals than we do today. To help provide context on the attitudes toward animals in a given era, each chapter of this book begins with a period-specific development in that ever-changing bond, whether it be the creation of commercial pet food or the growing animal rescue movement. Pet history is part of American history. No person stands outside of their cultural moment, not even the American president.

With our ever-changing culture, one thing remains constant in the United States: politics has always produced bitter debate and sharp division among Americans. A political system based on the competition of ideas often tends toward vitriolic partisanship. As the history of presidential pets is largely divorced from policy, it offers us a chance to see our leaders, past and present, as people rather than politicians. Whatever one might think of George W. Bush's foreign policy or Joe Biden's infrastructure package is irrelevant in this context, where their obvious love for their dogs illuminates oft-obscured aspects of their personalities. During the writing of this book, I found myself gaining a surprising amount of sympathy for presidents whose policies I strongly oppose. Of course I am not the first person swayed by a cute furry face. Herbert Hoover used a photo of his dog to help win his election, and Richard Nixon saved his political career by invoking his daughters' puppy, Checkers, during a nationally televised speech. Having a dog does not make you a better president, but the way a person (even a president) interacts with a dog can make that person relatable to a dog-crazy public.

On a personal level, I am in a good position to understand the way dogs can help people forge connections. As a legally blind man, I have traveled with a black Labrador retriever named Sammy for the last seven years. He is an invaluable and necessary part of my life. While I rely on him to guide the way, Sammy also acts as a crucial point of connection to the world. We cannot enter a restaurant or a grocery store without comment, and strangers often approach me to talk about their own furry friends. There is a bond between dog owners, a link that feels personal even when it isn't. Working with a guide dog makes you a de facto ambassador for disability education. I regularly find myself explaining service animals to children who have never encountered them and then happily discussing pet care with their parents.

Shortly after being paired with Sammy, I was offered a chance to work for the Presidential Pet Museum, an online collection of history and lore covering the full gamut of First Pets. I would be lying if I said my own relationship with animals wasn't part of my interest in the specific swath of history covered by my work for the museum and my writing of *All-American Dogs*. The behind-the-scenes details of life at the White House, the hours offstage when presidents and their families are at their most "normal"—these are the details that can bring color and perspective to history. Learning that the single most powerful person in the country, an individual whose pronouncements can impact global finance and whose command can launch potentially apocalyptic nuclear strikes, is still worried about a puppy pooping on the rug is my version of the old "he puts his pants on one leg at a time" cliché. What dog person can't relate?

To the serious history buff, it might seem trivial to discuss a politician's pet ownership. I would argue that presidents' private moments directly impact their ability to make decisions. Anyone who has tried to run a conference call or write a memo with a barking dog in the room can easily understand how this might be. Likewise, every person who has enjoyed a few minutes petting a puppy on a stress-filled day can appreciate the clarity such moments of reduced anxiety can offer. The recent rise in the number of animals trained to provide emotional relief for people suffering from post-traumatic stress disorder bears this out, as do several examples in this book. Presidents under great pressure—Lincoln during the Civil War and Kennedy during the Cuban Missile Crisis, among others—interacted with dogs to relieve the burdens of office.

The human-animal relationship runs both ways, of course. Just as dogs make our lives easier, we must likewise help them. To this end, the reader can find a list of resources at the end of this book. It contains just a small sampling of the many wonderful organizations working to improve the lives of animals, from rescue shelters to animal rights advocates. No such list is exhaustive, but this one offers a variety of ways to improve an animal's life.

Beyond my personal interest and my desire to draw attention to worthy causes, I hope this book offers readers a new perspective on American history. By tracing the evolution of presidential dog ownership, we gain insight into a president's thought processes. Just as important, we expand our understanding of the world in which those presidents lived. It is possible to replace the carved-in-granite images of distant historical figures with three-dimensional flesh-and-blood people. Far from being trivial, this shift in perception is exactly why the study of history exists in the first place.

1

FOUNDING DOGS

JUNO AND SATAN
Mixed Breeds

Whatever America's founders may have thought of global supremacy or the pomp with which today's presidents are treated, they would not have been surprised by the presence of dogs in modern political life. Dogs have been at the side of world leaders for centuries. In China, the Pekingese, thought to resemble a lion, was a court staple during the Han Dynasty, which ran from 206 BCE to 220 CE. Charles II, who ruled Great Britain from 1660 to his death in 1685, was so fond of his toy spaniels that he tolerated their constant disruption of his court, prompting one of his courtiers to grumble, "God save your majesty, but God damn your dogs!" His relationship with his pets was so well-known that a breed of dogs, the King Charles spaniel, bears his name. William III, the celebrated monarch of the seventeenth century, famously loved pugs, and for good reason. His great-grandfather William the Silent had been saved from assassination by the barking of his beloved pug, Pompey. Ever the proud dog lovers, William III and his wife, Mary II, brought a pug with them when they traveled from Holland to England to accept the throne. During their reign, the pug became inextricably linked with the British monarchy.

Researchers believe dogs arrived in North America by crossing the Siberian land bridge over 9,000 years ago. They were common in indigenous communities prior to the arrival of Europeans. Of course, as settlers traveled west to colonize the New World, they brought their own dogs with them, adding to the canine variety on the continent. By the mid-eighteenth century, dogs were everywhere in colonial life. They were used for hunting, for herding livestock, and for

Much like their modern counterparts, dog lovers of the eighteenth century considered their canine companions a key part of their identity. While the average American colonist kept mixed-breed dogs around the house, the wealthy bred their own pets and even commemorated them in portraits.

companionship. Those traveling to the New World brought this pro-canine culture with them. More important, they brought their own dogs. That colonists cared for their canines is evident in newspaper advertisements offering rewards for the return of lost pets and in tributes written to those dogs who had died. Ben Franklin, the foremost chronicler of colonial life, wrote in 1738, "There are three faithful friends—an old wife, an old dog, and ready money."

Around this time, wealthy English on both sides of the Atlantic began to prize purebred dogs, who became a symbol of one's elevated station. Any commoner could own a mixed breed mutt—certainly there were plenty of available pups roaming the back alleys looking for scraps of food—but only the most refined could spend time and money carefully cultivating desired traits in their canine companions. Dogs were bred for hunting, racing, and fighting. The brutal practice of baiting—in which dogs were forced to fight bulls, bears, or other animals for the amusement of paying customers—gained popularity in Great Britain during this time. Different tasks required different traits, and the careful selective breeding that accentuated these traits resulted in a number of different dog breeds arising from the gene pool.

The Old English bulldog arrived with British colonists and took hold primarily in the southern states, where its tenacity and strength made it an ideal match for the feral hogs who had arrived in the New World with earlier settlers and had no natural predators in North America. A number of different "shepherd's dogs" could be found throughout the colonies, and they were prized for their attentiveness and their protective instincts regarding livestock.

Dalmatians, often known as coach dogs, were a status symbol, bred for their beautiful spotted coats. Their comfort around horses led to their most famous role, as firefighting dogs. Dalmatians often raced toward fires ahead of the swift horses pulling the firefighting equipment, clearing a path for colonial first responders. When not racing to fires, they were used to guard the firehouse, protecting the equipment from thieves.

It isn't surprising that an American president, the face of a fledgling republic, would own dogs. At a time when only landowning men could vote and a hot trend among wealthy landowners was owning purebred dogs, the odds were fairly good that the nation's chief executive kept at least a few. George Washington, ever the model of overachievement, proved to be more than your typical wealthy connoisseur.

GEORGE WASHINGTON

In Office: 1789–1797

POLITICAL PARTY: FEDERALIST

George Washington remains, after two and a half centuries, one of the most revered Americans. His successful pursuit of the American Revolution and his stabilizing role as America's first president have rightly guaranteed a special place for him in the history of the United States. Unlike his brilliant but volatile aide Alexander Hamilton, his brilliant but gruff vice president, John Adams, or his brilliant but overly idealistic secretary of state, Thomas Jefferson, Washington possessed the subtle dignity and political skills to bind together a fractious group of states into a nation greater than the sum of its parts.

The so-called Father of His Country understood his role, not only in his own time but in history. Every decision, every action, set a precedent for future presidents. While his most significant action in this regard was his choice to retire after a second term, allowing the peaceful transfer of power to his successor Adams, it

The first American president, George Washington, had a complex relationship with dogs.

is worth noting that Washington was also a dog lover. Thirty of the presidents who came after him have followed in that tradition.

Washington's fascination with canines did not begin during his time in office. By 1772, he could, according to his friend Bryan Fairfax, distinguish superior and inferior pups in a litter generally considered to be excellent. This is not surprising. For most of his life, Washington ran his own breeding program at Mount Vernon and took careful notes about each litter and its origins. Evaluating the results of each canine union was critical to the success of his efforts.

When George Washington assumed the office of president of the United States on April 30, 1789, there was no White House. The location of the nation's capital remained an undecided issue and a controversial topic at the time of the inauguration. Some members of Congress believed it should be New York City, others supported Philadelphia, and representatives from every state lobbied for their own region's worthiness as a capital. The seat of power initially rested in New York City, then shifted briefly to Philadelphia before finally settling on the Potomac River. The American experiment with democracy wobbled unsteadily in the aftermath of the Articles of Confederation, and few, if any, would have predicted a future where America dominated the globe culturally and politically. Instead, the optimists among the 10,000 people who attended the first inaugural parade in New York City hoped a stable government could be developed from the recently adopted Constitution, proving that democracy was more than a utopian philosophy.

More than 230 years later, we find ourselves steeped in a culture with an elaborate symbolic iconography surrounding the presidency. We have spent

General Lafayette leaves Mount Vernon, the estate of his good friend George Washington, in 1784. Within a year, he would send a collection of French hounds to improve Washington's breeding program.

our entire lives looking at images of the White House, its Rose Garden and grounds, the red carpets blanketing its staircases, the bright natural light of the Oval Office. We have seen presidents fly in and out on Marine One, the presidential helicopter. And more important for the purposes of this book, we have seen presidents, in all these magisterial settings, with their dogs.

During Washington's presidency, the District of Columbia was little more than a marshy patch of wilderness on the Potomac. The iconic buildings we associate with American democracy were barely completed blueprints. The Executive Mansion remained incomplete until 1800, by which point Washington had passed away. Instead, much of Washington's time in office was split between New York City, Philadelphia, and Mount Vernon. At each stop, he had canine companions.

Elizabeth Willing Powel, wife of Philadelphia's mayor Samuel Powel, recalled meeting Washington during the First Continental Congress, when Washington was walking his dog Sweet Lips, whom he described to Mrs. Powel as a "perfect foxhound." The Virginia planter proudly told her that he had bred the dog himself. The two developed a friendship, and she brought him to the attention of her husband and other powerful men. Years later, when the U.S. government briefly resided in the City of Brotherly Love, the Powels often hosted President Washington for lavish dinners. Elizabeth Powel was among the confidants who convinced Washington to run for a second term as president. As in our modern era, strong bonds could be forged while walking your dog.

Mount Vernon, the Virginia estate on which Washington primarily resided, was also home to dozens of dogs spanning a variety of breeds. Existing records show that the estate held spaniels, terriers, Dalmatians, hounds—you name it. Almost every breed of dog in North America during the late eighteenth century had a representative on the general's farms. Many of these dogs had unusual names. Madame Moose was a coach dog. Drunkard, Tipsy, Tippler, and the aforementioned Sweet Lips were hounds.

Most of the dogs at Mount Vernon worked in one way or another. The terriers killed rodents that might otherwise have destroyed stores of grain and other foods. The spaniels helped flush out land birds during hunts, making it easier for Washington and his slaves to obtain meat for the dinner table. Hounds aided the regular fox hunts with which Washington filled his winter months. Coach dogs—most likely Dalmatians—rode along with the president as he traveled.

Even though his duties took him away from home on a regular basis, Washington took a strong interest in his dogs, visiting the kennels every morning when he was home. He was also very focused on the breeding of his dogs, especially the hounds, which he continually sought to improve through selective pairings. Washington felt that his hounds needed an increase in speed, and he worked to build a superior hunting dog.

In 1785, his beloved friend and Revolutionary War compatriot the Marquis de Lafayette sent seven aggressive French hounds as a gift to Washington. The dogs traveled from their native France in the care of a young John Quincy Adams. Unfortunately, it seems Adams didn't take his duty as courier as seriously as he should have. The ocean voyage took weeks, and the dogs were known for their assertive (to put it mildly) behavior, so perhaps the future

George Washington returns from a hunt with his faithful dogs.

president had seen enough by the time the ship docked. Upon arrival in New York, he left the hounds at the port rather than accompanying them to their new owner.

This dereliction of duty displeased Washington, but the hounds did not. They were larger than his own hounds, and so ferocious that a slave was assigned to monitor their feedings so they did not attack one another. The president soon bred them to his existing stock. The resulting dogs were the forebears of the American foxhound.

The new breed of hound was faster and more aggressive than earlier ones. These qualities improved the hunt but could occasionally cause trouble in other circumstances. On the evening of a grand feast, one of the French hounds, Vulcan, stole the magnificent ham procured for the occasion. When Martha, the president's wife, asked why that evening's dinner did not include the expected main course, she was informed of Vulcan's successful kitchen raid. The guests reportedly chuckled softly, but Washington laughed heartily. Martha was less than amused.

While most of the dogs lived in kennels, it is believed that some were kept in the mansion itself. This was not uncommon in eighteenth-century America, particularly during the winter months, although as warm weather brought fleas and ticks that could not be contained, dogs routinely moved outside in the spring and summer.

Washington's kennels burned down in 1792. Worried that his hounds had decimated the deer population on his estate, the president opted not to rebuild, effectively ending his breeding program.

Unfortunately, any discussion of George Washington's relationship with dogs must include some much darker actions. As a slave owner, our first president lived with paranoia and the suspicion that the people he kept in bondage were secretly undermining his estate. In this case, he believed that the dogs belonging to his slaves were being used to steal from his livestock to supplement the diets of their owners. In a letter dated December 16, 1792, President Washington wrote to his overseer Anthony Whitting: "If any negro presumes under any pretence [*sic*] whatsoever, to preserve, or to bring [a dog] into the family that he shall be severely punished, and the dogs hanged." What Washington meant by "severely punished," we are left to imagine.

He was not alone in these dark practices. His secretary of state, Thomas Jefferson, carried out similar dog-killing campaigns on his plantation at Monticello. This cruel practice may have temporarily reduced the loss of livestock, but eradicating the dog population among slave communities proved impossible.

In an interview with the author, Mount Vernon research historian Mary V. Thompson suggested the origin of these contraband canines is up for debate: "We don't know where they came from." However, she explained, enslaved people "had small garden plots and could sell the vegetables, fruits, chickens, and eggs that they raised for themselves." This allowed slaves some money, which could be used to buy dogs. It is also possible that such produce could be traded directly for a dog. Even among slaves who did not have goods to sell or trade, it seems likely that stray dogs would have been commonplace and easy to take in.

The dogs belonging to Washington's slaves would most likely have been of mixed breed and therefore not the type of animals he would have wanted breeding with his personal canines, whose breeding was carefully monitored and controlled. When interbreeding between "true" dogs and curs occurred, the resulting puppies were drowned. This horrific practice was not uncommon and continues among some disreputable breeders even today.

What to make of George Washington, dog owner? As with Washington the historical figure, we must acknowledge both his tremendous accomplishments and his startling failures. To create an entirely new breed of dog is a monumental achievement, one unique among American presidents. Certainly, Washington cared deeply for his dogs and valued them greatly. Sadly, his love of animals did not extend to the mutts produced from unplanned pairings or to the dogs belonging to the enslaved people on his estate. Slavery, the foundational evil that helped build the American republic, poisoned everything it touched, even animal husbandry. We may wish this to be otherwise, but we cannot allow our celebration of Washington's best qualities to displace any mention of his worst.

JOHN ADAMS
In Office: 1797–1801

POLITICAL PARTY: FEDERALIST

While John Adams's dogs did not reside at the Executive Mansion for very long, they do own the distinction of being its first canine inhabitants. Theirs were the first muddy paws to sprint up the stairs, the first barks to echo through its hallways, and the first bladders to mark the grounds as the territory of presidential pets.

President John Adams brought a dog named Satan to the White House and lost his bid for reelection weeks later. Coincidence?

The second president of the United States lacked the unifying charisma of his predecessor, George Washington, and his sole term as the nation's chief executive was marred by political division and infighting within the administration. John Adams, a renowned Boston attorney, had been a pivotal figure in the Continental Congress during the debate over declaring independence. During the American Revolution, he served as ambassador to France. He spent eight years as vice president before winning election in 1796.

During his tenure as president, Washington, D.C., remained an undeveloped backwater, still more wilderness than bustling metropolis. The Executive Mansion, not yet dubbed the White House, remained under construction until Adams's first (and only) term was almost over. He moved into his new home in early November 1800, losing his bid for reelection shortly thereafter. Hopefully, he hadn't really unpacked before the election results arrived.

Adams and his wife, Abigail, brought two mixed breed dogs to the capital with them—Juno and Satan. Little is known about either dog's appearance or personality, although the First Lady, ever the letter writer, does mention Juno in her correspondence.

"If you love me," she wrote to her granddaughter, "you must love my dog." Clearly Abigail would have thrived in the sound-bite-focused media of the twenty-first century, where this sentiment would be emblazoned on coffee mugs, T-shirts, and bumper stickers in the online store of her husband's reelection campaign. Certainly her love for canines can be understood by dog owners across the political spectrum.

Her letter continued: "You will be glad to learn that Juno yet lives, although like her mistress she is gray with age," adding that Juno

First Lady Abigail Adams possessed a deep fondness for her dog, Juno.

"appears to enjoy life and to be grateful for the attention paid her. She wags her tail and announces a visitor whenever one appears."

Juno was clearly a good dog, but what to make of Satan? Did he live up (down?) to his name? We have no idea. Clearly, President Adams was not worried about bad publicity related to his pet's name. After all, it had been just over a century since the Salem Witch Trials, which left nineteen dead for less obvious connections to the devil, so a Massachusetts resident naming his dog after the devil feels like a daringly sick joke.

Considering that much of the election of 1800 revolved around the supposed atheism of eventual winner Thomas Jefferson, it's surprising that Adams's diabolical best friend wasn't used against him. In our modern era, a major candidate running for the presidency would certainly draw fire from cable news pundits for naming a pet thus. At the very least, Twitter would lose its collective mind for a few days speculating on the moniker's significance. Regardless, Satan marked his territory as one of the first dogs in the White House. Whether he had to sell his soul to his diabolical namesake for the honor remains unclear.

JAMES MONROE
In Office: 1817–1825

POLITICAL PARTY: DEMOCRATIC-REPUBLICAN

After the brief tenure of Juno and Satan, dogs did not reappear in the president's mansion for more than a decade and a half. Thomas Jefferson, who did have some dogs on his estate, Monticello, preferred the company of mockingbirds. At the time, it was common in Europe to train mockingbirds to sing opera. Given that Jefferson had been the ambassador to France for many years, it is probable that his favorite mockingbird, named Dick, could sing some arias. James Madison, who succeeded Jefferson, fled the Executive Mansion with his wife, Dolley, and her green parrot shortly before the British torched it. The white paint used during the repair of the building gave the president's home its now-familiar name, the White House. Dogs finally returned with James Monroe.

James Monroe's presidency coincided with what historians call the Era of Good Feelings. During this time, the Federalist Party, which

The last president of the founding generation, James Monroe presided over the Era of Good Feelings, a rare moment of national unity. His daughter kept a dog in the Executive Mansion.

had not held the presidency since John Adams left office in 1801, collapsed. For a brief period, the nation seemed headed toward unity and the elimination of political parties. Monroe purposefully included members of the dying Federalist Party in his cabinet and sought to downplay divisiveness.

The Monroe administration added Florida to the United States, shepherded the country through the Panic of 1819, and implemented the Missouri Compromise on slavery, which admitted Missouri to the Union but limited slavery to territory below the parallel 36°30' north. His greatest legacy is likely the Monroe Doctrine, which held that the United States would not allow European nations to interfere with newly independent nations in the Western Hemisphere.

Monroe had come of age during the American Revolution and served in the Washington administration. His presidency is seen as the last of the so-called Virginia Dynasty, when four of the first five American presidents hailed from that state. His term in office can be viewed as the end of an era in American politics, as those who had fought for independence handed the reins of power to the following generation with the election of John Quincy Adams in 1824.

At the time of Monroe's inauguration in 1817, his daughter Maria was fourteen. At some point during her time in the White House, Maria obtained a spaniel. George Tucker, a judge who visited the Monroes, mentioned the dog in a letter to his daughter. "She had a small Spaniel dog, with whom she was continually engaged in a trial of skill & the general opinion was . . . that she turned & twisted about more than the Spaniel." We do not know the specific breed of spaniel belonging to Maria (and it is even possible Judge Tucker mis-identified the breed), nor do we know the pup's name. As with John Adams's dogs, we are left with only a few tantalizing tidbits of information.

2
HOUSE-DIVIDED DOGS

FIDO
Yellow Mutt

The United States has never been more divided than it was during the Civil War, when over 600,000 Americans died fighting to settle issues related to slavery that the founders had left for future generations to resolve. Though combatants in the war might have been loath to admit that any bond connected them, it's clear that both northerners and southerners deeply valued animal companionship. Dogs (and sometimes other animals) served alongside soldiers as mascots, and their experiences are scarcely less harrowing than those of their human counterparts.

Among the most famous mascots was Jack, a mutt who belonged to a Confederate jailer until soldiers from the North were captured and the dog decided that he preferred the company of the Union prisoners. He left the jailer and traveled with his new friends to a prisoner of war camp in Salisbury, North Carolina. Released from the camp as part of a prisoner exchange, Jack traveled to Union-controlled Fortress Monroe, where a reporter from *Harper's Weekly* met the mascot and decided to tell his story in that magazine—highlighting the dog's switched alliances as a show of animal wisdom.

During the long march toward the prison camp, Jack performed duties common to many canine mascots—tasks that certainly helped endear him to the men and earned hard-to-come-by rations—finding both water and food (small game or, on a good day, stolen chickens) for his comrades. On a deeper level, the friendship and loyalty provided by an animal mascot helped cheer soldiers on both sides through unpleasant weather, grueling travel, and desperate battles.

The Richmond Howitzers, a group of artillerymen, kept a dog named Stonewall. During roll call, Stonewall joined the line like any good soldier, sitting on his haunches. The soldiers valued their mascot so much that if battle conditions forced them to change positions, they transported him in a chest. In this way, they ensured that he would not be lost or killed during the chaos of fighting.

Not every Civil War mascot was a dog, of course. A regiment of volunteers from Wisconsin famously traveled with a bald eagle named Old Abe. The eagle attended dozens of battles and skirmishes, flying above the rebel army and screeching. Though sharpshooters often attempted to bring him down, Old Abe survived the war and lived out the rest of his days in the Wisconsin State Capitol.

The use of dogs as mascots represents a deepening of Americans' relations with their animals. Whereas earlier generations related to animals most commonly as workers—dogs for hunting, cats as rodent control, horses for transportation—by the mid-nineteenth century, animals gained symbolic power that transcended friendship and utility. A dog (or an eagle) could represent the best qualities of a group of men, and perhaps even the nation.

During this era, many presidential incumbents did not have a dog, preferring other companions. John Quincy

During the Civil War, an eagle named Old Abe served as a mascot for Company C of the 8th Wisconsin Volunteer Infantry Regiment. He survived the war and is shown here at a celebration of America's 1876 Centennial.

Adams, whether distancing himself from his father's diabolical dog Satan or still traumatized from ferrying ferocious French hounds for George Washington, did not have a dog. John Quincy's wife kept silkworms at the White House, so these were likely the only creatures who could be considered pets in this administration. (While this may seem odd to us today, during a brief period in the first half of the nineteenth century, harvesting silk became a fad throughout the northeastern United States.)

It is rumored that the Marquis de Lafayette, he who previously sent Washington the seven hounds, brought Adams an alligator while Lafayette was traveling through the United States during John Quincy Adams's single term. Allegedly, this alligator lived in a White House bathtub. As alluring as this story may be, it is not supported by contemporary accounts and is likely apocryphal.

Andrew Jackson's two terms in office dramatically changed the presidency, creating the spoils system of political appointments and proving the lasting appeal of a common man as a presidential candidate. Jackson's great wealth may have placed him distinctly in the upper class, but his tough-edged frontier manners and history of dueling appealed to a majority of voters, who saw him as one of them. Jackson, combining both his aristocratic status and his unpolished reputation, kept a pet parrot named Pol who developed a strong proficiency for profanity, having heard so much from the president. The parrot even had to be removed from the president's funeral when his obscenities disrupted the proceedings.

Jackson's handpicked successor, Martin Van Buren, attempted to carry on Jacksonian policies, but lacked the charisma and common touch of his predecessor. He also lacked a swearing bird. A story persists that the Sultan of Oman gave Van Buren tiger cubs, but this did not happen. Van Buren was given a lion and a lioness, which were delivered to the consulate in Morocco. They destroyed part of the office and were sold at auction. Horses, the actual gift from the Sultan of Oman, were likewise auctioned off in accordance with the Constitution's emoluments clause, which prohibits a president from accepting valuable gifts from foreign leaders.

William Henry Harrison's time in Washington was brief—little more than a month—and much of it was marred by illness, as he battled pneumonia and eventually died. While Harrison had no dogs, the man who succeeded him eventually would.

JOHN TYLER
In Office: 1841–1845

POLITICAL PARTY: WHIG/INDEPENDENT

John Tyler arrived at the White House a widower with no pets of any kind. His tumultuous, unplanned presidency set a key governing precedent, but it took a May-December romance to restore dogs to the Executive Mansion.

Tyler's tenure as vice president proved brief, as President Harrison died one month into his term. Tyler immediately took the oath of office and assumed the mantle of the presidency. Eventually the president was expelled from the Whig Party by that party's members of Congress. Opponents of Tyler referred to him derisively as "His Accidency," but Tyler claimed that the vice president was the natural choice to complete a fallen president's term. In taking this stand, he established a precedent for presidential succession, one that would be followed several more times before the ratification of the 25th Amendment in 1967.

At the time of his controversial inauguration, Tyler was a widower. However, in 1844,

John Tyler, the first vice president to assume the presidency upon the death of his predecessor, was also the first president to get married while in office. He gave his new bride two dogs.

OTHER TYLER DOGS

President Tyler also gave Julia a pair of Irish wolfhounds. Like their much smaller kennelmate, these dogs were imported. Tyler, a wealthy landowner prior to his election, had no qualms about the cost of such gifts and likely saw the rarity of these breeds in the United States as symbolic of both his status and the special nature of the love he felt for his young wife. Unlike Le Beau, the wolfhounds remain largely unknown to us. No specific details of their lives remain today. We don't even know their names. In this sense, they share a similar fate with President Tyler, who remains little remembered by the American people as a whole and poorly regarded by most historians. His proslavery views and his post-presidential decision to join the Confederacy during the Civil War overshadow his main contribution to American culture—the ascension of vice presidents into the role of fully empowered presidents in the event their predecessors cannot serve a full term.

he married Julia Gardiner, a woman thirty years his junior (and five years younger than his eldest daughter). The president soon gave his new wife an Italian greyhound procured by the American consul in Naples. This dog, named Le Beau, was allegedly quite a handful.

After arriving in New York following his transatlantic journey, Le Beau spent a few weeks with Julia's mother in New York before making the final leg of the journey to the capital. Mrs. Gardiner wrote to her daughter, "I think a great deal of him, but I would not take such a pet for a gift." Perhaps the puppy was not housebroken, or perhaps the stress of such a demanding voyage caused Le Beau to misbehave.

Once in the White House, Le Beau continued his antics. The First Lady replied to her mother that her new puppy required "attention and discipline." It seems he was hard on both the furniture and the rugs in the Executive Mansion. Still, she claimed in the same letter, "Little Le Beau is perfectly well and hearty and has the most unfailing attention." These statements at first seem contradictory, but it appears the dog felt a deep devotion to his people and demanded the same in return.

FRANKLIN PIERCE
In Office: 1853–1857

POLITICAL PARTY: DEMOCRATIC

The fourteenth president of the United States, Franklin Pierce, was the first to receive dogs as a gift from a foreign leader, and those puppies formed one of the few bright spots in his administration. Following three presidents—James Polk, Zachary Taylor, and Millard Fillmore—whose only animal companions were horses, Pierce came to Washington without pets and overwhelmed by grief.

Tragedy struck in early January of 1853, when the train car occupied by president-elect Pierce and his family derailed. While Pierce and his wife, Jane, survived, their young son perished in the crash, sending both parents into a severe and prolonged depression. While the president put on a brave front and moved forward with the formalities and duties demanded by his office, Mrs. Pierce retreated from public view for nearly two years.

Pierce, understandably, was not looking for a pet. However, the diplomatic efforts of his predecessor, Millard Fillmore, to open relations with the long-isolated country of Japan brought more to America than increased trade. The emperor of Japan, in a gesture of goodwill, sent President Pierce seven small dogs. These tiny pooches—most likely a breed known as the Japanese Chin—were called "sleeve dogs," because they could easily fit inside the sleeve of a kimono.

The establishment of diplomatic relations with Japan was a major coup for the United States, as the East Asian kingdom had closed its borders to foreigners over two centuries before. The treaty between the United States and Japan (negotiated by Commodore Matthew C. Perry) allowed the United States access to new goods as well as to a new consumer market. It also launched Japan into the Industrial Age, which indirectly led to the Japanese imperialism that eventually resulted in World War II.

Pierce and his contemporaries could not have predicted such consequences. Just over the horizon loomed a civil war that the president tried to avoid, largely by appeasing the South. His cabinet contained several notable southern politicians, including his secretary of state, the eventual Confederate president, Jefferson Davis.

Davis's wife Varina gives us the most detailed description of the tiny dogs gifted by the Japanese emperor. They had, she said, "a head like a bird with a blunt beak, eyes large and popped, and a body like a newborn puppy of the smallest kind." President Pierce presented one of the dogs to Secretary Davis. The very day the dogs arrived in Washington, Pierce hurried to the Davis home, announcing, "Gen-

The presidency of Franklin Pierce began in personal tragedy and ended in political failure. Pierce did get to keep a puppy given to him by the Japanese emperor, though.

eral, I have a dog for you!" Jefferson Davis reportedly loved the dog—which he named Bonin—so much that he carried his new pet around in his pocket.

Pierce kept one of the dogs for himself and gave the others to friends. History does not record what happened with the president's tiny canine companion, but Pierce himself served only one term. His party declined to renominate him, choosing James Buchanan instead. The nation moved closer to secession and conflict; Pierce moved back to New Hampshire. He remained a controversial figure until his death in 1869, when he died of cirrhosis after a long struggle with alcoholism.

JAMES BUCHANAN

In Office: 1857–1861

POLITICAL PARTY: DEMOCRATIC

Rankings of the presidents of the United States, whether by historians or the public at large, consistently place James Buchanan near the very bottom of the list. Though as a dog owner he helped popularize the Newfoundland breed in the United States, Buchanan is no one's favorite president. The fifteenth president's unwillingness to confront slavery, the dominant issue for most of his term, or to quell the secession of the southern states, which overtook his final months in office, solidifies his abysmal reputation.

There are many reasons to dislike Buchanan as a historical figure, and certainly his deliberate inaction contributed to the wholesale slaughter of the Civil War. His single term in office remains a low point in American history, an era of bad feelings with almost no redeeming value.

Except for the dogs.

Lara, Buchanan's Newfoundland, weighed a reported 170 pounds, possibly making her the larg-

President James Buchanan loved his Newfoundland, Lara.

ANOTHER BUCHANAN DOG

Buchanan never married, and he remains the only bachelor president ever to serve the United States. In the absence of a wife to fulfill the duties of First Lady, he brought his niece Harriet Lane to Washington, D.C., with him. Harriet brought with her a toy terrier called Punch—so named because the dog could purportedly fit under a downturned punch bowl. Why one would trap a dog in that fashion is not explained. Buchanan did not like Punch very much. In letters sent to Harriet during one of her travels, he remarked that he was trying to avoid the terrier, who remained at home, as much as possible. The toy terrier and the Newfoundland—one minuscule and one behemoth—shared the same spaces at the White House and must have made an interesting pair, assuming they interacted in any meaningful way. We have no reports of their adventures, though certainly they must have served in their positions as First Dogs more ably than their master did in his. How could they not? In March of 1861, President Buchanan, his niece Harriet, and the two mismatched pooches returned to Wheatland. He did not run for reelection, much to everyone's relief.

est dog to ever call 1600 Pennsylvania Avenue home. Buchanan had acquired her a couple of years before he became president, shortly before leaving the country for a tour as minister to Great Britain, which lasted from 1853 to 1856. He missed Lara dearly, and she held a prominent position at Wheatland, his estate in Lancaster, Pennsylvania, upon his return.

Reporters for *Frank Leslie's Illustrated Newspaper* visited Wheatland in 1856 as part of their campaign coverage. In a March 1857 article, they describe Lara, misidentifying her gender:

*Prominent also [at Wheatland] is Mr. Buchanan's Newfoundland dog
Lara, remarkable for his [sic] immense tail and his attachment to his
master.*

Lara slept next to the president while at the White House, and true to her
breed, she took on the role of his personal protector. Visitors often remarked
that she seemed to sleep with one eye open. Certainly, given her size, anyone
intending to harm the president would have had second thoughts. Lara's dark
coat and gigantic stature reminded some of the president's friends of a bear.

In the late 1850s, Newfoundlands were a relatively rare breed in the United
States. Their popularity grew in the subsequent decades, and eventually
Faithful, another Newfoundland, arrived at the White House with Ulysses S.
Grant in 1869.

*Buchanan's
dog, Lara, as
depicted in*
Frank Leslie's
Illustrated
Newspaper *in
March 1857.*

ABRAHAM LINCOLN
In Office: 1861–1865

POLITICAL PARTY: REPUBLICAN

Abraham Lincoln loved animals. Born with profound empathy, he held views about them that were remarkably progressive for the mid-nineteenth century, particularly in the frontier territory of Illinois. As a boy, Abe adopted a neighbor's piglet, caring for it until it became an adult. When his father butchered it to feed the family, young Lincoln refused to eat any part of the animal. Around this time, he also gave up hunting of large game after the killing of a wild turkey filled him with regret. He seemed incapable of cruelty.

At a time when dogs were often treated with casual indifference by their owners, Lincoln took a different approach. In 1855, he acquired Fido (Latin for "faithful"), a yellow mutt. Fido joined the Lincoln home and served as a devoted friend for Abe, then a lawyer on the rise socially and politically. Having a pet signified ascension to the middle class, but Fido was far from a superficial status symbol. The dog was indulged and granted freedoms that would be unusual even today.

Modern standards of obedience (as well as leash laws and other restrictions on canine behavior) were unknown in Springfield. Training pet dogs was unusual in the 1850s. Thus the dog roamed freely through the city, usually with Mr. Lincoln or one of the boys. Prior to the 1860 election, when Abe remained clean-shaven, Fido often accompanied him to the local barbershop.

During work hours, the dog was welcome at Lincoln's law office but usually played with the children. Fido routinely ate his meals with the family by begging from Lincoln and his boys, Willie and Tad. Mary Lincoln disliked Fido's tendency to track mud into the home, particularly as the dog often joined the boys in bed, but her husband treated animals and children with great forbearance.

After the lackluster presidencies of Franklin Pierce and James Buchanan, the American Experiment appeared close to an end. The election, in November 1860, of the rough-hewn, antislavery Lincoln resulted in several southern states preemptively seceding from the Union. The three-fifths compromise made during the Constitutional Convention in 1787 had long ago

Abraham Lincoln is considered the GOAT by many presidential historians. During his time in the White House, he also owned two goats—Nanny and Nanko.

solidified southern dominance over national politics by according states with large slave populations additional congressional representation and more electoral votes. But a split between northern and southern Democrats allowed the young Republican Party to claim victory. The election results infuriated legislators in South Carolina, and they vowed to leave the Union. Soon other southern states followed. President Buchanan did nothing to end the uprising, and tensions continued to escalate.

As he prepared to leave his home in Springfield, Illinois, for the White House, Lincoln sought advice from various esteemed politicians and worked to construct a cabinet equipped to handle the coming difficulties. As he deliberated upon a course forward that would save the nation, he took time to find a new home for the faithful Fido.

Upon news of Lincoln's victory, supporters had swarmed the president-elect's home, singing songs, cheering, and setting off fireworks and cannons in celebration. The ruckus terrified Fido, who hid behind the sofa, trembling. The dog, Lincoln surmised, would have difficulty with the weeks-long trip to the capital and the clamor of the family's new home. Lincoln wanted to ensure that his dog would be treated well, so he made arrangements for the pup to live with his close friend John Roll, whose boys often played with Willie and Tad. To ensure his beloved companion's comfort, Lincoln delivered Fido's favorite horsehair sofa and a set of strict guidelines along with the dog. Fido was to be fed table scraps, and he was never to be tied alone in the backyard. Whenever the dog scratched at the door, he was to be allowed entrance. The new owners were never to scold Fido for having wet or muddy paws. Most important, the dog would retain his freedom of movement throughout the city.

After the Lincolns moved to Washington, Fido became a sort of mascot for the city of Springfield. He continued his usual life, wandering as he pleased, eating from the table, and leaving muddy paw prints in his wake. Both the Lincolns and the Rolls viewed this as a temporary arrangement; Fido would return to life in the Lincoln home when the president's time in office ended and he returned to Illinois for retirement.

In November 1864, Lincoln became the first president since Andrew Jackson to win reelection. He lived long enough to see the end of the Civil War, celebrating after rebel forces surrendered in early April 1865, but died from an assassin's bullet days later, barely a month into his second term. The president's murder shocked the country, even many former Confederates, and

This is the first known photograph of a presidential dog, Abraham Lincoln's Fido.

resulted in an outpouring of grief that briefly unified the polarized and already reeling nation. Lincoln's body lay in state at the White House before returning to Springfield via train. The Roll family took Fido to the Lincoln home, where mourners were gathered, to honor the fallen president.

It's likely that the surviving photographs of Fido—the first ever taken of a presidential pet—were produced after the assassination, as souvenir hunters swamped Springfield searching for Lincoln memorabilia. The photos would have been a popular item for grief-stricken tourists to take home. Fido, the beloved Lincoln pet and town mascot, became a commodity.

Unfortunately, the free-range lifestyle Lincoln guaranteed for his furry friend led to disastrous results. Fido, long accustomed to cheerfully greeting people by jumping and placing his paws on them, finally accosted the wrong person. Charles Planck, a Civil War veteran known as a drunk, did not take well to Fido's muddy-pawed salutation, and he stabbed the dog for dirtying his clothes. Fido fled

ANOTHER LINCOLN DOG

President Lincoln did not live the dignified, mud- and dander-free political life his wife would have preferred. He acquired a number of pets, filling the White House with cats, goats, a turkey, and another dog. The new pup, Jip, lunched with the president on most days. The Civil War took a severe emotional toll on Lincoln. His daily meals with Jip and the other pets (he was known to feed cats from the table as well) offered some comfort during the darkest, bloodiest years in American history.

in pain, retreating to a local cemetery, where he was found days later, dead. Like his former master, the president who sought to end America's bloodiest war "with malice toward none," Fido died at the hands of an assassin unwilling to accept the offer of friendship.

President Lincoln's love of animals, from pigs to dogs, feels surprisingly modern. While not a vegetarian, he displayed a sensitivity to cruelty that sets him apart from most of his contemporaries. The most redeeming quality of some presidents is their pet ownership, but Lincoln manages to add his admirable kindness toward all living creatures to a list of accomplishments few, if any, presidents have matched.

3

RECONSTRUCTION AND GILDED AGE DOGS

GRIM
Greyhound

As the Civil War and its aftermath were transforming American life, an American named James Spratt was busy in London, transforming relationships between humans and dogs. Spratt, who had crossed the Atlantic to sell lightning rods, noticed something strange at the London docks: dogs loitered near the ships and devoured the old hardtack discarded by arriving sailors. Hardtack, a cracker made with flour, water, and salt, provided a shelf-stable food source for seamen on their long journeys. Spratt realized that he could manufacture a version of the maritime biscuit for canine consumption. All he needed was a market.

In 1860, Spratt's Patent Meat Fibrine Dog Cakes became the first commercially available mass-produced dog food ever manufactured. The cakes were composed of grains, beetroot, vegetables, and "the dried unsalted gelatinous parts of Prairie Beef." Spratt erected one of the first color billboards, advertising his biscuits by depicting a Native American buffalo hunt, with the obvious implication that his dog cakes contained bison meat. (Whatever the public may have inferred from his ads, until his death Spratt remained secretive about the food's actual meat source.)

Spratt's dog food cost the equivalent of a day's wage for the average skilled craftsman, so he aimed his ads squarely at well-to-do English gentlemen, who could afford the new food, trusting that as the upper class began to buy the new product, upwardly striving members of the middle class would follow. He also pioneered the life-stages marketing commonly used by pet food manufacturers today, creating different products for puppies, young dogs, and seniors.

By 1870, Spratt had opened operations in the United States. The dogless presidency of Andrew Johnson had ended in disgrace and the triumphant Civil War hero Ulysses S. Grant occupied the White House. America was still rebuilding, fighting over how to remake itself in the aftermath of its ghastliest war. The rise of industry, particularly in the North, fostered a growing middle class with enough disposable income to afford items like Spratt's, which they had not known that they needed or wanted before. In the United States, Spratt targeted attendees of dog shows and members of kennel clubs, again betting that interest in the product would trickle down to people of more modest means after it was adopted by the wealthy. In 1889, Spratt's bought the entire front cover of the first-ever journal of the American Kennel Club.

Prior to the spread of commercial dog food in the United States, most Americans fed their dogs table scraps or low-cost horsemeat. Little thought was given to the long-term health consequences of the average canine diet. Spratt's masterful marketing changed that. By the late nineteenth century, canine diets were much more widely discussed, though scientific research and government regulation could not keep pace with fads. For example, some Gilded Age dog owners refused to give their dogs meat, fearing it would cause the animals to revert to the wild ways of their undomesticated forebears.

The major political issues of the day—civil rights for African Americans, the Reconstruction of the South, and civil service reform—dominated American politics and consumed the waking hours of the era's presidents. When they needed a break from the grind, however, all of the period's presidents (except for

Chester A. Arthur) had at least one dog around to lighten the burdens of office. We don't know if any of these pups ate Spratt's dog cakes, but any dog able to relieve the tensions of the chief executive certainly deserved the best.

CAUTION.—It is most essential that when purchasing you see that every Cake is stamped SPRATT'S PATENT, or unprincipled dealers, for the sake of a trifle more profit, which the makers allow them, may serve you with a spurious and highly dangerous imitation.

SPRATT'S PATENT
MEAT FIBRINE DOG CAKES.

From the reputation these Meat Fibrine Cakes have now gained, they require scarcely any explanation to recommend them to the use of every one who keeps a dog ; suffice it to say they are free from salt, and contain ''dates,'' the exclusive use of which, in combination with meat and meal to compose a biscuit, is secured to us by Letters Patent, and without which no biscuit so composed can possibly be a successful food for dogs.

Price 22s. per cwt., carriage paid; larger quantities, 20s. per cwt., carriage paid.

"Royal Kennels, Sandringham, Dec. 20th, 1873.
'' To the Manager of Spratt's Patent.
''Dear Sir,—In reply to your enquiry, I beg to say I have used your biscuits for the last two years, and never had the dogs in better health. I consider them invaluable for feeding dogs, as they insure the food being perfectly cooked, which is of great importance "Yours faithfully, C. H. JACKSON."

'' 36, North Great George Street, Dublin, June 9th, 1874.
'' Gentlemen,—Please to forward to my private residence, as above, 4 cwt. of Dog Biscuits as before ; let them be precisely the same as those supplied on all former occasions I have much pleasure in bearing personal testimony to their suitability and general efficiency for greyhounds, and in adding that my greyhound, Royal Mary, winner at Altcar of last year's Waterloo Plate, was almost entirely trained for all her last year's engagements upon them. "Yours obediently, WILLIAM J. DUNBAR, M.A."

'' Rhiwlas, Bala, 21st June, 1873.
'' Sir,—I have now tried your Dog Cakes for some six months or so in my kennels, and am happy to be able to give a conscientious testimonial in their favour. I have also found them valuable for feeding horses on a long journey, when strength and stamina are important objects. It was the opinion of my brother judges and myself that dogs never appeared at the close of a week's confinement in better health and condition than the specimens exhibited at the Crystal Palace Show, and I understand that your Cakes are exclusively used by the manager. "R. J. LLOYD PRICE."

This logo appeared on advertisements for Spratt's Patent Meat Fibrine Dog Cakes in the 1800s. The company created the market for commercial dog food, convincing pet owners to buy special biscuits rather than feed their dogs leftovers.

ULYSSES S. GRANT
In Office: 1869–1877

POLITICAL PARTY: REPUBLICAN

Ulysses S. Grant came to the presidency after his victory in the Civil War. As one might expect of a nineteenth-century military commander, Grant favored horses above other animals. This did not mean, however, that he didn't love dogs. In his two terms at the White House, we know of two canine friends who lived on the grounds.

After the disastrous (and dog-free) presidency of Andrew Johnson, the electorate threw its support behind Grant, the general who had led the Army of the Potomac and overseen the surrender of Robert E. Lee's Confederate forces less than four years before. Grant faced the difficult task of rebuilding the war-devastated South while also working to aid and protect the millions of African Americans freed from bondage. At the same time, the country continued to expand westward, coming into conflict with the native peoples of the American West. These were not insignificant is-

Civil War hero General Ulysses S. Grant was elected president in 1868, after the disastrous term of Andrew Johnson.

An engraving of General Ulysses S. Grant and his family,
circa 1868, shortly before he entered the White House.

sues, and like many anxious Americans, President Grant needed the company of a dog to help him cope.

Grant had four children, and his youngest son, Jesse, was eleven when the general assumed the presidency. Jesse had a Newfoundland, appropriately named Faithful, who moved with the family to Washington, D.C. Several Newfoundlands belonged to presidents in this era. They were known to be good with children, as well as protective of their families. The president loved his children, and he was particularly careful with the feelings of his youngest child, whose previous pets had lived tragically short lives. According to legend, President Grant threatened to fire the entire White House staff if the boy's dog suffered an untimely demise. While we don't know much about Faithful, there were no recorded mass firings during Grant's eight years in office, so it seems likely that the dog survived both terms.

RUTHERFORD B. HAYES
In Office: 1877–1881

POLITICAL PARTY: REPUBLICAN

The single-term presidency of Rutherford B. Hayes marked a shift in the way American presidents talked about animals. A devoted dog owner, President Hayes was the first chief executive to use the office to openly advocate improvements in animal welfare.

The election of 1876, between Democrat Samuel Tilden and Republican Hayes, proved incredibly close. As the votes were counted, there were twenty electoral votes in dispute. Tilden needed only one to win, but Hayes required all twenty. Eventually, a backroom deal handed Hayes the White House in exchange for an end to the nation's efforts at Reconstruction. The military would no longer occupy the states of the former Confederacy, but Hayes and his dogs would occupy the Executive Mansion.

Lucy Hayes, the First Lady, refused to serve alcohol in the White House. Critics referred to her derisively as "Lemonade Lucy." Her principled stand may have been unpopular

President Rutherford B. Hayes's dog Grim met a fate worthy of the name.

in the salons attended by Washington's entrenched elite, but it underscored the reform-minded policies of her husband, who vowed to serve only one term.

Both President Hayes and his wife loved animals deeply. The president used the weight of his office to speak out against animal cruelty in 1878 during his annual address to Congress, what we now refer to as the State of the Union Address. "The abuse of animals in transit is widely attracting public attention," he noted. He urged Congress to consider "the enactment of more efficient laws for the prevention of these abuses." These comments raise no eyebrows in our modern world but were considerably more radical in the late nineteenth century.

Hayes's love of animals did not prevent him from hunting; two of the dogs he brought to the White House were hunting dogs named Juno and Shep. We don't know very much about these dogs—even their breed is a mystery—but their presence highlights the complexity of ethical issues regarding the treatment of animals.

The most well-known of the many Hayes pets was Grim, a greyhound who joined the family courtesy of Mrs. William DuPont of Wilmington, Delaware, when he was two years old. "He is good-natured and neat in his habits," the president noted in his diary, "and took all our hearts at once." The other dogs did not immediately appreciate the newcomer—their noses were "out of joint," in the president's words—but eventually he became fully integrated into the family.

Unlike hard-drinking politicians, Grim loved the First Lady. He displayed particular excitement when she returned from any significant period of absence. The greyhound's desire to accompany Lucy extended to music as well. Once, as she sang "The Star-Spangled Banner," he began to howl along. He must have received an approving response, as thereafter he continued to "sing" along to the national anthem whenever Mrs. Hayes would sing it.

True to his word, Rutherford B. Hayes served only one term as president. In 1881, he moved his family and their many pets home to Spiegel Grove, Ohio. Grim, much like Abraham Lincoln's Fido, had the run of the town. He roamed the streets and did not yield for oncoming carriages. Instead, they turned for him as he stood his ground. Grim evidently enjoyed the privilege that came with being a former president's beloved companion.

First Lady Lucy Hayes, President Rutherford B. Hayes, and their dog Duke.

Unfortunately, as the nation evolved from a rural and agrarian society into an industrialized one, Grim fell victim to the changing times. He died after being struck by a train. While no one is certain why the dog did not move, the president concluded that Grim must have expected that the locomotive, like any other vehicle, would stop for him. The family mourned the dog's death.

Perhaps their grief was somewhat tempered by two puppies that had joined their lives since leaving the nation's capital. The puppies had been fathered by the late, beloved Grim.

OTHER HAYES DOGS

The arrival of Hector, the Hayes family's Newfoundland, highlights the mid-nineteenth-century popularity of the large breed at 1600 Pennsylvania Avenue. While neither Jesse Grant's Faithful nor Hayes's Hector was apparently as large as James Buchanan's 170-pound Lara, Hector must have been an imposing figure for any White House visitor to encounter. Hector seems to have been a well-behaved giant, but we know very little about him. No record of playful destruction or misbehavior exists.

The Hayes family had a number of other dogs, including Dot (a cocker spaniel), Duke (likely an English mastiff), Otis (a miniature schnauzer), and Jet (breed unknown). They also had three cats (including a pair of Siamese), a mockingbird, and a goat. Clearly, these were serious pet lovers. The president wrote to his daughter that the large number of animals gave "a Robinson Crusoe aspect to our mode of life."

JAMES A. GARFIELD

In Office: 1881

POLITICAL PARTY: REPUBLICAN

The presidency of James Garfield lasted only six months, and for a third of that time Garfield lay dying from an infection caused by inept medical responses to an assassin's bullet. By all accounts, Garfield possessed a towering intellect and a compassionate spirit. His untimely death renders his term in office a tragic what-if for historians. What he might have done to advance civil rights or to reform the civil service (the two major issues of the day), we will never know.

We do know, however, that Garfield had a Newfoundland named Veto, who lived with him for two years prior to Garfield's election in 1880. The dog received his name in honor of Rutherford B. Hayes's objection to a bill abolishing the marshal of elections, as Garfield shared the then-president's antipathy to the legislation.

The dog also, it seems, sought to assist Garfield in his correspondence. An 1881 report from the *Chicago Tribune* shared this story:

> *He had written nearly the whole of the first page when "Veto," who had been standing by wagging his tail for some time, and trying to get some attention from his master, at length became impatient, and placed his big, dirty paw upon the page still wet with ink, and*

made an unreadable and unsightly scrawl of the whole. "O you good-for-nothing old fellow!" said [Garfield], patting the dog's head, "you have made me a good deal of trouble and labor by your over-familiarity." He then quietly tore up the sheet, and began his letter again.

Garfield held no presidential ambitions and could not have foreseen how fitting a name Veto would be. The Republican convention of 1880 featured several prominent contenders but no clear favorites for the presidential nomination. After a grueling series of votes in which no candidate could secure the necessary support, Garfield's name was offered as a compromise choice, and the stunned Civil War general found himself the Republican candidate for the White House.

Throughout the nineteenth century, the preferred style of campaigning for the presidency involved staying at home and letting reporters and supporters come to you. The Garfield family farm transitioned overnight into a combination of tourist attraction, media circus, and campaign headquarters. Political allies visited, reporters and souvenir seekers roamed the estate, and each night brought torchlight gatherings of admirers. Veto did not enjoy the sudden influx of strangers tromping through his territory.

Contemporary press accounts indicate that the large dog would wander among the crowds, growling and barking, showing his displeasure. After being admonished for this behavior, Veto begrudgingly accepted the presence of the multitudes. However, upon Garfield's election, the family decided that the dog was ill suited for the hustle and bustle of life in the White House. Veto, the family decided, would remain on the farm rather than travel to Washington, D.C.

James Garfield assumed the office of the presidency at noon on March 4, 1881. On July 2, he was shot by Charles J. Guiteau, an unhinged office seeker. For a time, it seemed the president would survive the assassination attempt. The bullet did not contact any vital organs and could have remained in his body. Unfortunately, American physicians had yet to accept germ theory, and various doctors poked and prodded the president's wound with bare fingers and unsanitized probes. Aside from the horrific pain such procedures caused the wounded Garfield (who was not anesthetized), they also resulted in sepsis, which eventually killed him.

President James Garfield worried that his Newfoundland, Veto, would be unable to handle the stress of life in the White House. Garfield's term ended in tragedy when he died from infection after an assassination attempt.

Of course Veto, not having made the trip to the White House, could not have known of his master's fate, but a June 1882 article from the *Dover Weekly Argus* suggests that something snapped within the dog around the time of the president's demise.

One sultry Sunday, [Veto] came into the house with bloodshot eyes and acted wholly unlike himself. The young Garfield boys were at Mentor then, and fearing that the dog would bite them, Rudolph went after a gun to kill him. By the merest accident, the dog escaped death, and the next day was given to a farmer from Mayfield, who took him away at once.

Fortunately, Veto recovered from the supposed derangement, and while his personality had reportedly changed from the earlier, pre-presidential days, he was no longer considered a danger. In fact, there are two stories of canine heroism attributed to the dog in his life after Garfield's death.

The farmer who adopted Veto was J. H. Hardy. The dog took to his new family and soon resumed his protective behavior. Veto slept in the barn, and he refused to allow anyone other than his family to touch the items stored there. Moreover, he seemed to view himself as responsible for the behavior of the animals he shared quarters with.

In one instance, a horse became agitated and got loose during the night. Veto howled until Mr. Hardy woke and headed to the barn to see why the dog was raising such a ruckus. There he found Veto standing, holding the horse's bridle in his mouth, preventing further damage until the larger beast could be calmed.

On another occasion, Veto raced to the home of a sleeping neighbor, barking and scratching at the door of the quiet house until everyone within was awakened. This rude alarm angered the neighbors until they noticed flames coming from their barn, which was quite near their house. The noisy and observant dog had saved their lives, if not their barn.

Among presidential dogs, Veto is by far the most heroic, even if he never had the chance to live in the Executive Mansion. How, then, do we process his reportedly dangerous behavior following the death of the president? Was he driven "mad" by grief? Was he just having a bad day? We will never know, but his narrow escape from euthanasia likely saved the lives of a family years later.

GROVER CLEVELAND
In Office: 1885–1889, 1893–1897

POLITICAL PARTY: DEMOCRATIC

In 1905, some years after his second term as president of the United States concluded, Grover Cleveland wrote an article about hunting for a publication called *The Independent*. In it, he describes the thrill of a rabbit hunt: "The baying of three or four good dogs steadily following a little cotton tail should be as exhilarating and pleasant to the ears attuned to the music as if the chase were for bigger game." The obvious enjoyment the former president got from the howls of his dogs indicates a fondness for canines. That we know so little about his specific pets is regrettable.

Cleveland is best remembered over a century later as the only president to serve nonconsecutive terms, with his time in office interrupted by the four years of Benjamin Harrison's administration. Cleveland was the first Democrat elected to the presidency since the disastrous term of James Buchanan ended in 1861.

He holds other distinctions as well. A bachelor when elected, he married the twenty-one-year-old Frances Folsom in the Blue Room at the White House on June 2, 1886, making him the first (and thus far only) president to marry in the White House. The couple's second daughter, Esther, was the first child born there.

In order to protect his young family's privacy, Cleveland bought a large working farm in Georgetown, and he spent most of his time there, rather than in the Executive Mansion. (The family resided at 1600 Pennsylvania Avenue only during the busiest months of the social season, in November and December.) The privacy afforded to the president's wife and children extended to the family dogs, too.

In 1893, the United States consul serving in Bremen, Germany, sent the First Lady three dachshunds—then a relatively rare breed in the United States. The *New York Times* documented their arrival, noting the arduous 4,000-mile journey the dogs had taken to their new home. In 1894, a *Chicago Daily Tribune* correspondent noted the presence of wild hares on the White House grounds. Certainly, the dachshunds would have enjoyed chasing them. (Another cocker spaniel is also mentioned in this article, as are game chickens and exotic goldfish.)

President Cleveland, who entered office a bachelor, left it surrounded by a

President Grover Cleveland owned a number of dogs, but they lived away from the Executive Mansion.

large family and an even larger menagerie of animals. In his later years, long after the hares at the White House excited his dachshunds, he continued to hunt, his ears remaining attuned to the music of baying hounds.

OTHER CLEVELAND DOGS

GALLAGHER AND MILLIE: During the four years of Benjamin Harrison's term (1889–1893), the Clevelands bought a home along Buzzards Bay in Massachusetts. A *New York Times* reporter visited the out-of-power Cleveland there and encountered two dogs: Gallagher, a cocker spaniel, and Millie, a fox terrier. "Both animals take great liberties with Mr. Cleveland when he is accessible to them," the reporter noted, "and when not otherwise employed are rolling each other about on the lawn." Other dogs called the Massachusetts estate home, including two prizewinning specimens, a Saint Bernard and a poodle.

KAY: Not much is known of President Cleveland's Saint Bernard, Kay. Reportedly, she was a prizewinner and lived at the family's Massachusetts home.

HECTOR: This French poodle belonged to Mrs. Cleveland, but he had a troubled reputation. The *Chattanooga Daily Times* described him as "a great reprobate" who "wanders all over town at all sorts of hours of the night." Poodles are highly intelligent and sometimes strong-willed creatures, so perhaps this is not surprising. However, calling the president's dog a "reprobate" feels like what soon became known as yellow journalism, the reporting of sensationalized or exaggerated news.

BENJAMIN HARRISON
In Office: 1889–1893

POLITICAL PARTY: REPUBLICAN

During the single term of Benjamin Harrison, the White House was filled to capacity. The president and his wife, Caroline, were joined in the residence by her father, two of their adult children and their spouses, a number of grandchildren, a goat, two opossums, and a handful of dogs. This marked a significant change from Harrison's predecessor—and eventual successor—Grover Cleveland, who had purchased a Georgetown estate to house his family.

The sheer size of the extended Harrison clan makes it difficult to determine the ownership of the various animals at the White House during that time. The opossums, named Mr. Reciprocity and Mr. Protection after key planks in the Republican platform of the day, were gifts from the president to his grandchildren. Old Whiskers, the family's goat, likely belonged to the president's

During President Benjamin Harrison's time in office, the White House was filled with children and animals.

son, Russell. The dogs' allegiances are generally unknown, as are their names. The one exception is a collie mix named Dash.

Like the opossums, Dash had been a gift from the president to his grandchildren, though the dog seems to have preferred the president's company. Harrison liked the dog well enough to order the construction of a fancy doghouse just for Dash next to the Executive Mansion. Harrison's affections had limits, though, as the president worried that his peers would think less of him if he played with Dash too often.

This sensitivity might not have been unfounded. An 1891 article from The *New York Times* bemusedly remarks on the Harrisons' fondness for plain Indiana cooking rather than more sophisticated fare. Though the president was the grandson of President William Henry Harrison and the great-grandson of founding father Benjamin Harrison V (a signer of the Declaration of Independence), his midwestern roots made him an outsider to the upper crust of the nation's capital. His large extended family and their wild menagerie no doubt added to this schism.

During his term, Harrison oversaw the addition of six new states to the Union, as well as the passage of the Sherman Anti-Trust Act. He also had the White House wired for electricity, although he and his wife were so afraid of accidental electrocution that they allowed the lights to burn all night, preferring that a skilled technician turn them off in the morning.

Harrison's refusal to utilize the spoils system for the benefit of the Republican Party angered many of the people who had supported him in 1888. At the same time, tariffs passed during his administration caused the prices of imported goods to skyrocket. The economy grew sluggish, sinking toward what would eventually become the Panic of 1893. While Harrison was renominated at the Republican Convention, he faced stiff cultural headwinds that made his reelection unlikely.

Caroline Harrison, the First Lady, died of tuberculosis two weeks before the 1892 election. The president, facing defection from members of his own party as well as the rise of the Populist Party in the western states, lost decisively to Grover Cleveland in a rematch of the 1888 election. The grandkids and dogs dispersed when he left the White House in 1893.

President Benjamin Harrison's son, Major Russell Harrison, with his daughter Marthena, nephew Benjamin "Baby," and niece Mary McKee, a dog, and Old Whiskers the goat. The president's grandchildren often rode around the White House grounds in this cart.

4
PROGRESSIVE ERA DOGS

ROLLO ROOSEVELT
Saint Bernard

Nature seemed to be on every mind at the turn of the twentieth century. City dwellers flocked to parks, hoping to find some refuge from the grind of metropolitan life. Yellowstone had recently become a protected space. John Muir and other supporters founded the Sierra Club. As the appreciation for nature grew, so too did a split in how writers approached discussing the natural world and animals in particular. Some writers anthropomorphized animals, endowing them with human characteristics and behaviors. Others sought to present a more scientific approach, with animals presented as purely instinctual beings.

Concern for the welfare of animals rose in the public consciousness with the 1890 publication of Anna Sewell's *Black Beauty*, a sentimental novel following the life of a horse as he is passed from owner to owner, some of whom are kind and some cruel. Sewell's purpose was not naturalistic; she wanted readers to evaluate their own treatment of animals and encourage legal reforms to protect creatures who could not protect themselves.

In 1903, Jack London published *The Call of the Wild*. London's novel tracks the life of Buck, a domesticated dog who is stolen from his California home and sold as a sled dog for use in the Klondike Gold Rush. As Buck faces increasingly grueling conditions, he sheds his veneer of civilization, giving into instinct, which not only enables him to survive but helps him become a leader among sled dogs. The novel's initial printing of 10,000 copies sold out almost immediately, and the book became a sensation. London followed his success with a sequel, *White Fang*, about a wild dog who slowly becomes civilized. It too was a success. Together, the novels, for good or ill, helped shape perceptions about canines—their intellect and their place in society. London employed a more observational approach than Sewell, though the work of writing adventure novels required some dramatic license.

The backlash to these and other successful works came with a 1903 article in *The Atlantic* by John Burroughs called "Real and Sham Natural History."

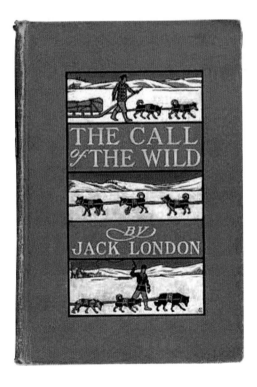

Jack London's The Call of the Wild *was an immediate bestseller upon its publication in 1903. The book remains popular today and is often used in middle and high school curriculums.*

Though Burroughs primarily attacked sentimentalized nonfiction ("the yellow journalism of the woods"), it wasn't long before popular fiction came in for criticism too. In 1907, President Theodore Roosevelt published his views in *Everybody's Magazine* under the title "Nature Fakers." While his focus was largely on those who fabricated details in nature writing, he also called out *White Fang* for what he deemed unnatural portrayals of animal behavior.

While literary criticism has traditionally been outside the purview of sitting American presidents, Roosevelt was uniquely qualified to address this issue. As the interest in conservation and the demand for animal-centered literature grew, it seems only fitting that Roosevelt should come to dominate the century's first two decades of American politics. An avid outdoorsman, a self-styled naturalist, and an insatiable pet owner, Roosevelt embodied the moment.

Roosevelt served not quite two full terms as president, but his ideas and actions loom over the entire era, impacting the administrations of both William Howard Taft and Woodrow Wilson. He represented a clean break from the quaint, reserved Republicanism of his predecessor, the assassinated William McKinley. The twentieth century, like Roosevelt, would move faster and speak louder. And like Roosevelt, every president for the rest of the century (with the possible exception of Woodrow Wilson) would have dogs in the White House.

THEODORE ROOSEVELT
In Office: 1901–1909

POLITICAL PARTY: REPUBLICAN

President Theodore Roosevelt nurtured a lifelong love of animals. An avid horseman and hunter, TR also owned more pets than any other president in U.S. history.

No president in the history of the United States has had more pets during his term than Theodore Roosevelt. During his time in office, his family had a lizard named Bill, a one-legged rooster, a badger named Josiah, a macaw, several snakes, flying squirrels, a pony, a kitten called Tom Quartz, guinea pigs, and several dogs. The rational observer might wonder why (or how) one family kept so many animals around. The answer, as with all questions relating to TR, lies in the personality of the man himself.

Theodore Roosevelt always loved animals. "As soon as I began to read at all," he recalled in an article called "My Life as a Naturalist," "I began to like to read about the natural history of beasts and birds and the more formidable or interesting reptiles and fishes." Born into a wealthy New York family, as a child Theodore suffered from severe asthma. His father believed that the best cure for the boy's illness was vigorous exercise. Young Theodore took his exercise outdoors when possible, and he used this time to collect animals he had read about in his natural history books. Sometimes he brought specimens home and performed his own taxidermy on them, much to the horror of the family maid.

The family's wealth allowed them to take trips abroad, and through hiking, boxing, horseback riding, and other outdoor activities, Theodore learned to control his body. This instilled a lesson he held dear for the rest of his life—that vigorous action was a requirement for a meaningful life. Certainly, few presidents have had careers as varied as his. He served in the New York State Assembly, worked as a cattle rancher, wrote books, led the New York City Police Department, served as assistant secretary of the Navy, fought in the Spanish-American War, won election as governor of New York, and became vice president—all by the age of forty-two. His political foes in the Republican Party had handed him the vice presidency as a way to neutralize him as a political force. In 1900, the year he served as running mate for President William McKinley, the position held no real power.

Everything changed—for Roosevelt and the United States—six months into his time as vice president when an anarchist named Leon Czolgosz shot President McKinley at the Pan-American Exposition in Buffalo, New York. Roosevelt had been on vacation in the Adirondacks but hurried to Buffalo as the president's condition worsened. McKinley died while Roosevelt was en route, and TR took the oath of office upon reaching the city. As his detractors had feared, he brought his thirst for action to the White House.

He also brought six children and a host of animals. Roosevelt encouraged his children's love of nature with the same forbearance his parents had shown him during his youthful days of amateur taxidermy. While he respected the decorum of the presidency and appreciated its symbolic value, he did not overburden the children or their pets with restrictions.

Theodore Roosevelt remains the only U.S. president to own a pet one-legged rooster.

At least two terriers belonged to the president's family—Blackjack (more commonly called Jack) and Skip. Though they were similar in stature, the dogs had little in common.

Jack was a purebred Manchester terrier who had been with the family since at least 1902, when the president sent a letter to Mrs. Roswell Field and included a photo of the pup with his son Kermit. The dog, he told her, was "absolutely a member of the family." First Lady Edith Roosevelt loved him dearly, as did the children. Though Jack occasionally chewed on books, it seems his main weakness was a fear of cats, particularly Tom Quartz, who habitually tormented the dog, pouncing on him until he ran away.

Three of President Roosevelt's dogs, shown here with two unidentified men.

Skip joined the family in May of 1905, after the president encountered him on a hunting trip in the western United States. Roosevelt wrote to his daughter Alice: "He is half fox terrier and half bull terrier and is as cunning as possible." Skip accompanied the hunting party, joining dogs of much larger size as Roosevelt and his companions hunted bobcats and bears. Though the little dog enjoyed riding on horseback with the president, he kept pace with the group even if refused a ride. "He is hard as nails," Roosevelt told his daughter in the same letter, certainly high praise coming from the battle-tested man of action. At night, the dog insisted on sleeping with the president, who eventually brought him back to the White House as a gift for his son Archie.

Skip adjusted well to the White House. While the president dearly loved Skip, the First Lady preferred the purebred Jack, who did not particularly enjoy Skip's company, either.

Sadly, Jack did not survive the entirety of Roosevelt's time in office, and the family buried him behind the White House. As the family prepared to leave 1600 Pennsylvania Avenue, Edith realized that there was one thing on the White House grounds she couldn't bear to leave behind—Jack. The dog's coffin was exhumed and transported to the Roosevelts' estate, Sagamore Hill, for reburial.

Roosevelt was an exceedingly popular president and likely could have won a second full term in office, but he had sworn not to run again after being reelected in a landslide in 1904. As the 1908 election neared, he threw his full support behind his friend William Howard Taft, who won the office that November.

True to his own philosophy, Roosevelt pursued vigorous action throughout his presidency. He oversaw the construction of the Panama Canal, became the first American to win a Nobel Peace Prize (for his diplomatic efforts to end the Russo-Japanese war), helped establish the national park system, and worked to improve working conditions for laborers. Certainly, he had many reasons to be proud. One achievement that certainly would have pleased the lifelong animal enthusiast came decades after his death, when a breed of dog was named for him. The Teddy Roosevelt terrier was standardized in 2019, a celebration of Roosevelt's fondness for terriers.

OTHER ROOSEVELT DOGS

SAILOR BOY: Sailor Boy, a Chesapeake Bay retriever belonging to the family, possessed what the president, according to his autobiography, considered "the strongest character." While Sailor Boy often served as peacekeeper among the many Roosevelt dogs, he still displayed the courage that the president valued so highly. The dog was "passionately devoted to gunpowder in every form, for he loved firearms and fairly reveled in 4th of July celebrations—the latter being rather hazardous occasions as the children strongly objected to any 'safe and sane' element being injected into them, and had the normal number of close shaves with rockets, Roman candles, and firecrackers."

PETE: While Sailor Boy worked hard to keep his fellow canines from fighting, his calm demeanor never quite rubbed off on the family's bull terrier, Pete. The rambunctious dog gained a reputation for nipping the heels of visitors to the Executive Mansion. On at least two occasions, the dog's territorial nature crossed the line from nipping to major aggression. When French ambassador Jean Jusserand visited 1600 Pennsylvania Avenue for some tennis with the president in 1906, Pete did not let more than a century of international cordiality dampen his spirits. He chased the ambassador, who escaped by climbing a tree. This incident led to Pete's exile to a farm in Virginia for roughly eighteen months. The president must have decided that lessons had been learned, because Pete eventually rejoined the family in Washington. On the morning of May 11, 1907, a Navy Department clerk drew Pete's attention. Like Jusserand before him, Thomas fled to safety in a tree. He lost part of his pants in the pursuit. Even for presidents who own badgers and allow their children unfettered access to fireworks, there are some limits. After this second incident, Pete went to Sagamore Hill, where the possibility for international incidents dramatically decreased.

MANCHU: Not all interactions with foreign governments went so poorly. In 1905, President Roosevelt sent his daughter Alice as part of a delegation traveling to Asia. While Secretary of War William Howard Taft negotiated a peace treaty between Japan and Russia, Alice distracted the press by smoking, staying out late, and spending time with Congressman Nicholas Longworth III. When the delegation arrived in Peking (now known as Beijing), Alice met with the empress dowager, Cixi, who honored the young American with a black dog later named Manchu. Likely a Pekingese, Manchu became a close companion for his mistress, who soon married Longworth and took Manchu with her when she left the White House.

ROLLO: When his friend Alfred S. Rollo offered the family a Saint Bernard in 1902, Roosevelt replied in a letter: "I am going to ask you not to think me churlish if I say we have three collies already, one of them a puppy, and four other dogs in addition, and that I really have not house room or stable room for any more." The president concluded: "I dare not venture to tell your proposition to my children." The children must have discovered the offer, as the dog, called Rollo after the president's friend, soon bounded through the White House with the other dogs.

WILLIAM HOWARD TAFT
In Office: 1909–1913

POLITICAL PARTY: REPUBLICAN

William Howard Taft won the presidency in November 1908 by running as Theodore Roosevelt's handpicked successor. Like his predecessor, Taft was an experienced politician with a progressive agenda built on busting trusts, but unlike TR, he kept his White House animals to a minimum.

For much of Taft's lone term in office, his family's only animal companions were two cows, Mooly Wooly and Pauline Wayne. These bovines provided milk for the First Family at a time when neither milk delivery service nor refrigeration was common, and they were more working animals than pets.

President Taft's wife, Helen—more commonly known as Nellie—was quite accomplished and set a number of precedents. She was the first wife to ride in her husband's inaugural parade and the first First Lady to support women's suffrage. She sometimes attended cabinet meetings, though she offered no opinions. She added after-dinner music to state dinners and helped arrange the planting of over 3,000 cherry blossom trees in the nation's capital. Nellie encouraged her daughter (also named Helen) to seize the opportunities denied women of her generation, and the younger Helen received a scholarship to Bryn Mawr.

Unfortunately, Nellie suffered a stroke in 1909, her husband's first year in office. Helen put her education on hold and joined her family at the White House, where she took over hostess duties during her mother's recovery.

During this period, the renowned opera singer Enrico Caruso performed for the Tafts at the White House. Caruso was one of the biggest celebrities of the era, in large part due to his early adoption of phonograph recordings. He recorded more than two hundred performances in his lifetime, garnering worldwide recognition and earning millions of dollars. His visit to the Tafts, therefore, is roughly equivalent to Elvis's meeting Richard Nixon, or perhaps Bob Dylan's performing for Barack Obama. Unlike Elvis and Dylan, Caruso arrived with a small white dog, which he gave to the president's daughter, Helen. In a show of gratitude, she named the dog after the singer.

President William Howard Taft owned fewer pets than many other presidents of his era, but he is notable for having the last cow to roam the White House grounds. Later presidents had milk delivered.

Caruso (the dog) lived a quiet life at the White House, even as President Taft's relationship with the perennially popular Theodore Roosevelt grew strained. Roosevelt began to advocate increasingly liberal policies, while Taft began to move to the right. Soon the two former friends were competing for the 1912 Republican nomination, which Taft eventually won.

During the general election, Roosevelt ran as a third-party candidate, effectively splitting the Republican vote and allowing New Jersey governor Woodrow Wilson to win the election. The Taft family left the White House, taking Caruso with them. No cows ever roamed the grounds of the Executive Mansion again.

WOODROW WILSON
In Office: 1913–1921

POLITICAL PARTY: DEMOCRATIC

Whether Woodrow Wilson owned dogs during his time in the White House is an open question. A century after the fact, we are left with clues and mixed messages, but few definitive facts. While it appears the president had a fondness for canines, it may not have extended to bringing a puppy to 1600 Pennsylvania Avenue.

President Woodrow Wilson is perhaps best remembered today as the commander in chief who oversaw U.S. involvement in World War I and pushed for an international League of Nations in that war's aftermath. Wilson believed in the spread of democracy and the potential for perpetual peace. These were lofty goals undermined by his virulent racism and support for Jim Crow policies in the United States. One of only two Democrats elected to the presidency between 1860 and 1932, Wilson was also the last president before the modern era of celebrity presidential pets.

As a young boy growing up in post–Civil War Virginia, Woodrow Wilson had a greyhound

Woodrow Wilson owned dogs during his lifetime, but did any of them reside at 1600 Pennsylvania Avenue?

named Mountain Boy. The dog appears in several sketches drawn by the future president. One of these currently hangs in the Woodrow Wilson House in Augusta, Georgia.

When Wilson entered the White House in 1913, he did not have a dog. He and his wife Ellen did have songbirds, but none of these achieved the public notoriety of Andrew Jackson's swearing parrot.

Ellen Wilson died of Bright's disease in August of 1914, little more than a year into Wilson's first term. After a period of depression, Wilson began courting a southern widow named Edith Bolling Galt, and they were married in December of 1915. (Wilson joins John Tyler and Grover Cleveland as the only presidents to marry while in office.) Edith did not bring dogs with her to the White House, nor did the president gift her with dogs, as Tyler and Cleveland did with their wives.

Some websites have reported that an Airedale terrier named Davie lived with the Wilsons around this time, and a photo of Wilson and Davie exists. However, a blog post on the Woodrow Wilson Presidential Library's website claims that Davie belonged to a family friend and not to the president. The blog cites a 1917 letter from *New York World* reporter H. E. C. Bryant to White House physician Cary T. Grayson as proof. The letter describes a dog named Davie, who has gone to live with a woman named Helen Bones. It is possible that the dog belonged to the Wilsons at one point and was later given to Ms. Bones.

By 1915, war had overtaken Europe, with the full might of industry now devoted to developing weapons that could kill on a scale previously unknown in combat. Machine guns, flamethrowers, tanks, U-boats, poison gases, and airplanes increased the slaughter to unprecedented rates. President Wilson promised to keep the United States out of the war and ran for reelection on that promise of peace in 1916. Shortly after his second inauguration, following the sinking of the RMS *Lusitania* by German U-boats, America joined the fight on the side of France and Great Britain.

American involvement in the war led to the arrival of Wilson's most famous pet—an unruly ram named Old Ike. As a public display of fiscal belt-tightening, Wilson replaced the White House grounds crew with a flock of sheep, freeing the gardeners to enlist in the armed forces. Old Ike was the lone ram at the White House, and he gained attention for his antics, which included chewing tobacco and eating the White House rosebushes. If any dogs lived with the president and his wife at this time, perhaps there are no definitive reports because Ike stole their glory.

World War I ended on November 11, 1918, and President Wilson traveled to Europe to help negotiate a plan for Europe's future. He favored an international League of Nations that would mediate disputes among member countries, thereby avoiding future war. In 1919, while touring the United States via train to drum up support for American involvement in the league, Wilson suffered a severe stroke, which left him largely incapacitated for the rest of his time in office. Edith and physician Cary Grayson secretly took on many of the president's obligations, and neither the public nor Congress was told the full extent of Wilson's health problems.

President Wilson's illness had kept him away from the spotlight, but an outpouring of support ensued later, when Wilson's presidency was over and his ailments were no longer hidden. After Wilson left the White House, one of the president's admirers sent him a bull terrier named Bruce. The dog had been specially trained for the ailing president. He was housebroken and a soothing presence. In modern terms, Bruce was a therapy dog, though dogs were not widely employed in that function for several decades after Wilson retired from office. Bruce lived with the former president, whose health never really recovered from the 1919 stroke, in a townhome in Washington, D.C., until Wilson's death in February 1924.

5

DOGS OF THE ROARING TWENTIES

KING TUT HOOVER
Belgian Shepherd

In the 1920s, eighty-three cents of every dollar spent on amusement was spent on movie tickets. Americans were movie-crazy; each week, 50 million tickets were sold, a number that represented almost half the population of the United States. During this time, with so many people going to the local movie palace so often, the biggest movie star of all was a dog named Rin Tin Tin.

Dogs were not new to cinema. The very first film shown to a paying audience, 1895's *Workers Leaving the Lumière Factory,* featured a dog mingling with the employees as they exited the building. A 1905 British film called *Rescued by Rover* became a sensation and was shown so often that the negatives deteriorated. (It had to be reshot *twice* to meet demand.) In the silent era, when human behavior could appear stilted on-screen as characters pantomimed to avoid speech, animals had a distinct advantage. They appeared natural and at ease on film, their behavior recognizable to audiences. Filmmakers built upon the growing cultural interest in nature from the previous two decades, and they moved dogs to the foreground.

Rin Tin Tin, affectionately known to fans as Rinty, came to the silver screen through highly unusual circumstances. In 1918, an American soldier, Lee Duncan, discovered a litter of German shepherd puppies in a kennel alongside fortifications the German army had recently abandoned. Most of the dogs housed there had died during an Allied artillery bombardment, but Duncan rescued five puppies and their mother, taking them back to his unit. He kept two of the pups and began training them, using a rubber squeaky toy as a reward for obedience. When the war ended, he managed to bring the dogs home and set to work training the male, Rinty, for the dog show circuit. When one of the shows was filmed, footage of Rin Tin Tin jumping over a twelve-foot hurdle caught the attention of movie producers, and the dog began appearing in films.

Prior to World War I, German shepherds were extremely rare in the United States. The breed had been developed at the end of the nineteenth century with an emphasis on attentiveness, courage, and physical strength, which made them

Many dogs worked alongside soldiers in World War I. Stubby alerted his human comrades to surprise mustard gas attacks, comforted the wounded, and participated in seventeen battles. He is the only American dog to attain the rank of sergeant through combat.

ideal for police and military work. During the Great War, every combatant nation except the United States employed dogs for various duties—from guarding the perimeter of an encampment to finding the still-living wounded on battlefields full of corpses to (regrettably) suicide bombing missions. The fact that Duncan found a kennel near a battlefield was not unusual.

Rin Tin Tin, the silent movie icon, often earned more money than his human counterparts.

As Americans returned from the war, they brought German shepherds with them. The dogs were prized for their loyalty and protective nature. When Rin Tin Tin began appearing in films, interest in the breed skyrocketed. By the end of the decade, German shepherds were ubiquitous in Hollywood—nearly fifty Rinty imitators tried (and failed) to overtake him at the box office. Shepherds even made it to the White House, where one lived with President Herbert Hoover.

The proliferation of media, from newspapers to film, and the relative prosperity of the postwar years allowed Americans to discover and purchase new breeds of dogs. As the public appetite for images of these canines grew exponentially, there emerged a new phenomenon: the celebrity presidential dog.

WARREN G. HARDING
In Office: 1921–1923

POLITICAL PARTY: REPUBLICAN

"Whether the Creator planned it so," Warren Harding once wrote in the *Marion* [Ohio] *Daily Star,* "or environment and human companionship have made it so, men may learn richly through the love and fidelity of a brave and devoted dog." The legacy of the twenty-ninth president of the United States—whose administration historians routinely rank with Andrew Johnson's and James Buchanan's as one of the worst in American history—is debatable. What cannot be doubted, however, is Harding's deep affection for dogs.

Harding, who owned the *Marion Daily Star* prior to winning the presidency, also possessed a keen understanding of publicity, and he kept his Airedale terrier, Laddie Boy, in the public eye. For a nation still reeling from the apocalyptic devastation of the Great War, regular updates on the life of the president's dog proved irresistible. Laddie Boy became the first celebrity presidential pet.

Warren Harding, a sitting senator from Ohio, won the Republican Party nomination in 1920. It was the first presidential election since the passage of the 19th Amendment, which guaranteed women the right to vote. Harding was charming and handsome, and his party's support of Prohibition and opposition to President Wilson's League of Nations helped him cruise to victory with 60 percent of the popular vote.

President Warren G. Harding with his Airedale terrier, Laddie Boy. While President Harding is not well regarded by historians, no trace of scandal taints his dog's legacy.

Harding and his wife, Florence, did not have a dog when they moved into the White House on March 4, 1921. Laddie Boy, a puppy who was born on July 26, 1920, at Caswell Kennels in Toledo, Ohio, arrived the very next day. The president ordered his staff to bring the dog to him immediately upon arrival, and Laddie Boy's appearance disrupted Harding's first cabinet meeting. For the rest of Harding's time in office, Laddie Boy would attend these meetings, and he had his own chair, like any cabinet secretary.

Airedale terriers are intelligent, having been bred for independent hunting. In the United Kingdom, they were used as military canines during World War I. They are occasionally referred to as the "king of terriers," as they are the largest dogs of that type. While their intelligence can make them stubborn and somewhat difficult to train, Harding appears to have had few difficulties. The *New York Times* reported that within a week of his March 5, 1921, arrival at the Executive Mansion, the president's puppy had learned to fetch the newspaper in the morning, bringing it to his master without incident.

Perhaps Laddie Boy simply wanted to brag about the media coverage he received. Both the *Times* and the *Washington Star* ran items about the dog almost daily. The president granted the media unprecedented access to his dog, and he rarely went anywhere without him. Laddie Boy was known to accompany Harding on golf outings, and he joined the First Lady at fundraising events. The dog's fame was such that Harding had a thousand miniature likenesses of Laddie Boy produced, and he gave them to supporters as souvenirs. These tiny Laddie Boys are now highly prized collector's items.

On rare occasions when the president felt his dog's media presence shrinking, he composed letters "from" Laddie Boy to major newspapers. In February of 1922, the *New York Times* published one such letter: "So many people express a wish to see me, and I shake hands with so many callers at the Executive Mansion," it read, "that I fear there are some people who will suspect me of political inclinations. From what I see of politics, I am sure I have no such aspirations."

For Laddie Boy's first birthday, Caswell Kennels sent him a bone-shaped cake. Accompanying this treat was a letter of encouragement "written" by the First Dog's father, Champion Tintern Tip Top. The letter expressed pride in Laddie Boy, whose antics were documented regularly in the local Toledo press.

The relentless press coverage spurred a public desire to own Airedale terriers, and the breed's popularity increased dramatically. Toy companies attempted to profit from the dog's popularity, and several contacted the White House seeking exclusive rights to an "official" Laddie Boy likeness, but the president refused to endorse any particular stuffed animals of his dog. Given the deep-seated corruption of many officials in his administration, this principled stand feels highly ironic.

By the summer of 1923, that corruption was catching up to Harding. His secretary of the interior, Albert Fall, had leased government lands to oil companies in exchange for personal loans. The press began to pursue the scandal—known as the Teapot Dome—as they had once pursued stories of the Hardings' dog. In an effort to distance himself from these ongoing troubles, President Harding traveled to the western United States and up to Alaska, then a U.S. territory. (He was the first president to visit Alaska, and he was photographed with a team of sled dogs while there.) During a stay in San Francisco, the president, who had not been feeling well for some time, died on August 2, 1923. The general public, who had been told days earlier that Harding had suffered gastrointestinal issues but was feeling better, was deeply shocked by his sudden death. The First Lady did not consent to an autopsy, but modern scholars believe he died from cardiac arrest. The nation, not yet fully aware of the corruption of Harding's administration, mourned deeply.

Laddie Boy had not joined his owners on their western excursion, and his handlers at the White House noted sadly that the dog awaited their return. The Associated Press reported:

> There was one member of the White House household today who could not quite comprehend the air of sadness which hung over the Executive Mansion. It was Laddie Boy, President Harding's Airedale friend and companion. Of late he has been casting an expectant eye and cocking a watchful ear at the motor cars which roll up on the White House drive. For, in his dog sense way, he seems to reason that an automobile took [the Hardings] away, so an automobile must bring them back. White House attachés shook their heads and wondered how they were going to make Laddie Boy understand.

A poet named Edna Bell Seward composed a poem called "Laddie Boy, He's Gone." ("Not alone, your dog's heart breaking for a glimpse of him again.") The poem was set to music by George M. Seward and was published

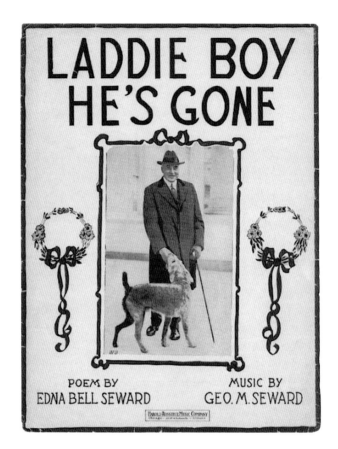

Imagine a nation grieving the death of a president, gathering around their pianos to sing mournful songs to the president's dog.

as sheet music so grieving Americans could gather in their parlors and sing condolences to the bereaved dog.

The nation's newsboys, in recognition of the deceased president's former occupation, collected pennies for a unique tribute to Harding. Nineteen thousand were collected and converted into a statue of Laddie Boy. (The dog, ever a good boy, sat for the sculptor, Bashka Paeff, on fifteen separate occasions.) The finished statue belongs to the Smithsonian but is not currently on display.

After her husband's death, Florence Harding gave Laddie Boy to Secret Service agent Harry L. Barker, whom she viewed as a son. Barker transferred to Boston when his White House service ended, and he took the iconic Airedale with him. Laddie Boy lived with the Barkers until 1929, when he passed away, reportedly of old age. The media darling once again made the papers. The *Times* reported that the dog passed with "his head on the arms of Mrs. Barker." The family buried him in Newtonville, Massachusetts.

Laddie Boy's legacy extends far beyond the decade in which he lived. His role as media darling set the stage for the much-loved presidential dogs to come—from Franklin Roosevelt's Fala to Barack Obama's Bo. The media attention Laddie Boy generated, cannily encouraged by President Harding, helped create the standard for presidential dogs, and it planted the idea of White House pets firmly in the popular imagination. Every subsequent animal to roam the living quarters of the Executive Mansion does so in the shadow of Laddie Boy. He remains President Harding's lasting contribution to American life.

CALVIN COOLIDGE
In Office: 1923–1929

POLITICAL PARTY: REPUBLICAN

Grace Coolidge, wearing an elegant red evening gown, stands in front of a blue background, her hand reaching down to Rob Roy, her white collie. The effect of her official White House portrait (painted by Howard Chandler Christy) is subtly patriotic and entirely transfixing. The timeless portrait of the First Lady dressed as if for a state dinner and accompanied by her loyal dog feels distinctly American. This painting, which currently hangs in the China Room of the White House, was reportedly beloved by Jacqueline Kennedy. It's not difficult to see why: both women were stylish, intelligent animal lovers, and both surrounded themselves with dogs.

Few presidents seemed to have loved dogs more than Coolidge.

Grace's husband, Calvin Coolidge, came to the presidency in August 1923, upon the untimely death of Warren Harding. Hailing from New England, Coolidge was a native of Vermont and became governor of Massachusetts before ascending to the vice presidency in 1920. At the time of Harding's death, a series of scandals arose, sullying Harding's reputation as president and his administration.

First Lady Grace Coolidge with her collie,
Rob Roy, in the only White House portrait to
feature a pet.

Coolidge, insulated by the then-insignificant role of vice presidents in the day-to-day workings of the executive branch, remained largely untouched by the controversies, and he helped restore respect for the presidency during his time in office. He believed in small-government conservatism, with the federal government taking a limited role in public life. Certainly this position stemmed from deep-seated philosophical conviction, but given the number of dogs (and other animals) the Coolidges kept during their stay in the White House, there may have been little time for interventionist governmental policies anyway.

"We always had more dogs than we could take care of," Calvin Coolidge admitted in his autobiography. No president has kept more dogs during his tenure than Calvin Coolidge. Even Theodore Roosevelt, whose menagerie exceeds all others', had only seven dogs. John F. Kennedy, who valued large families of people and pets, had ten dogs. The Coolidges had twelve. In addition to their dogs, Calvin and Grace also had several birds, two raccoons, two kittens, a donkey, and a bobcat. Small government, sure. Small vet bills? Nope.

Grace Coolidge held a special fondness for white collies, and certainly they are the dogs most often associated with the Coolidges. Rob Roy, immortalized in the First Lady's portrait, was purchased from a breeder in Oshkosh, Wisconsin, and originally bore the name of his hometown. Mrs. Coolidge changed his moniker, naming him after a popular cocktail (though this was the height of the Prohibition era). He was, as President Coolidge recalled in his autobiography, "a stately gentleman of great courage and fidelity" who led the way to the Oval Office each day. Prudence Prim, another white collie, joined the family after being purchased from Shomont White Collies in Monticello, Iowa.

President Calvin Coolidge loved Rob Roy as much as he loved small government.

Rob Roy slept in the president's bedroom every night, and both dogs regularly joined the family for meals. Humorist Will Rogers once visited the Coolidge White House, and multiple sources claim Rogers later remarked, "At one time, it looked to me like the dogs were getting more [food] than I was. I come pretty near getting down on all fours and barking to see if business wouldn't pick up with me."

While Rob Roy often attended meetings with the president, Margaret Truman reports that he disrupted only one gathering. At a crowded press conference, the dog suddenly began to howl. President Coolidge assessed the situation and said curtly, "Will you newspapermen kindly keep your big feet off my dog's toes?" Once the collie was given space, he quieted down.

The First Lady had calling cards printed for Prudence Prim, and whenever she visited someone, she would leave behind two cards—one for her and one for her beloved dog. The First Lady took full advantage of photo ops, and usually a white collie was involved. Prudence Prim's evident patience could only have helped endear her to the president and his wife. Once the dog was taken to a garden party wearing a straw bonnet decorated with ribbons and ferns. It was tied securely on her head, but she bore it well and undoubtedly charmed the guests in attendance.

Prudence Prim didn't love playing with all the Coolidge dogs, but she did enjoy scampering about with the family bulldog, Boston Beans. According to Margaret Truman, the collie would allow her short-legged companion to sprint, dragging his leash behind him; then she would grab the leash in her mouth, causing him to trip and fall. Fortunately for Boston Beans, he was never seriously injured.

In the summer of 1927, the First Family traveled to South Dakota for a three-month stay. They took Rob Roy, Prudence Prim, their chow Blackberry, and their pet raccoon, Rebecca. Prudence Prim died suddenly while in South Dakota. "We lost her in the Black Hills," the president recalled in his autobiography. "She lies out there in the shadow of Bear Butte where the Indians told me the Great Spirit came to commune with his children."

Rob Roy fell ill in September 1928, distressed by stomach problems. The Coolidges sent him to Walter Reed Army Hospital for treatment, to no avail. At the time, veterinary medicine focused more on cattle than on dogs and cats. That President Coolidge sent his dog to a human hospital for medical care shows both an unusual devotion and exceptional access to care regular Americans did not have. Their beloved collie died soon thereafter. Coolidge paid tribute to his dear friend, writing in his autobiography: "His especial delight was to ride with me in the boats when I went fishing. So although I know he would bark for joy as the grim boatman ferried him across the dark waters of the Styx, yet his going left me lonely on the hither shore."

OTHER COOLIDGE DOGS

PETER PAN: The first dog to join President Coolidge at 1600 Pennsylvania Avenue was Peter Pan, a wirehaired fox terrier with a white coat. Given to the Coolidge family by Dr. Alonzo G. Howard of Boston, Massachusetts, Peter Pan had an anxious temperament ill suited to life at the White House. In *White House Pets*, Margaret Truman wrote of Peter Pan: "He was not the friendliest of dogs. He snapped at people and in general showed a surly disposition." He tore off the skirt of a woman visiting the Executive Mansion, and he even disrupted one of the president's speeches by quarreling with another of the family's dogs. Eventually the president gave the terrier to his secretary, Edward T. Clark, one of the few people whose company the dog openly enjoyed.

PAUL PRY: No patience could be found within the Coolidges' Airedale terrier, Paul Pry. A brother to President Harding's beloved immortal Laddie Boy, he originally came to the Coolidge family with the name Laddie Buck. After a few days of observation, Mrs. Coolidge decided to change the name to Paul Pry. (Even a casual reader will note the First Lady's preference for an alliterative naming scheme by this point.) When questioned about the name change, Grace Coolidge replied that this dog had his snout in everyone's business. He certainly did not fill his brother's giant paw prints. Paul Pry attached himself to the First Lady and became overly protective. He bit a White House maid for attempting to enter the First Lady's bedroom. The family tried using a muzzle (a common practice in a time when many dogs roamed free), but Paul Pry's misbehavior worsened. The First Family eventually decided to give the terrier to a detachment of Marines known as the Devil Dogs. Even a group named after a diabolical canine found it difficult to manage Paul Pry, and he shuffled through a few more homes before landing at a navy yard and settling down to live out his days there.

TINY TIM AND BLACKBERRY: The Coolidge family had two chows, Tiny Tim and Blackberry. At the time these dogs joined the family, chows were uncommon in the United States, but photos of Tiny Tim spread quickly, prompting a surge of interest in the breed. Neither dog was very well behaved. Tiny Tim earned the nickname "Terrible Tim" for his antics. Blackberry howled incessantly, letting anyone within earshot know she was present. While President Coolidge could tolerate a fair amount of canine high jinks—his hands-off philosophy of federal oversight extended, it seems, to pet behavior as well—he could not handle Blackberry's constant baying. She was given to his daughter-in-law.

KING COLE: The departure of Blackberry left the Coolidges without a black dog, and breeder E. E. Spafford felt the president should own dogs of every color. King Cole, a Belgian sheepdog, greeted his new family with excitement, but it soon became apparent that he and Rob Roy were at odds. Mrs. Coolidge told the *Milwaukee Sentinel* that "King was born to be somebody's only dog, and he seemed always to be seeking for someone to love him and him alone." The family tried taking King Cole alone on a family trip, but this only agitated Rob Roy, who usually got to travel with the president. As President Coolidge's time in office wound down, the family gifted King Cole to a teacher from Kentucky.

BOSTON BEANS: Boston Beans, a small bulldog, wanted to lead the family's extensive pack, and he found Rob Roy's biggest weakness. Since arriving at the White House, Rob Roy had displayed a fear of elevators. Though he would ride with the president, he cowered and sometimes splayed himself on the elevator floor in a desperate bid to maintain his usual understanding of gravity. If Boston Beans happened to share the ride or be present when Rob Roy attempted to exit his mechanical nemesis, the bulldog would challenge the collie. This no doubt heightened Rob Roy's aversion to elevators. Given the collie's favored

(Continued)

position with President and Mrs. Coolidge, Boston Beans lost. The First Lady sent him to live with her mother.

CALAMITY JANE: Upon hearing of Prudence Prim's demise, two children from Michigan decided to send the president a Shetland sheepdog to ease his loss. Arrangements were made, and the dog traveled by plane to Washington, where she met the president as a white dog with black spots—or so it was assumed, until the black spots rubbed off on the president's clothing, and everyone realized she had gotten dirty en route. The almost entirely white (when clean) puppy loved to play, often becoming completely filthy in the process. In acknowledgment of the dog's mischievous nature, Grace Coolidge named her Calamity Jane, a reference to the trailblazing frontierswoman. President Coolidge, ever the practical New Englander, commissioned a canine bathtub to keep the newly christened dog clean.

PALO ALTO: In the early autumn of 1928, President Coolidge received an English setter bird dog named Palo Alto. Coolidge did not run for reelection in 1928, and he knew he couldn't take so many dogs with him into private life. Because English setters are active, headstrong dogs, the president decided that the White House (and his eventual retirement) were less than ideal for Palo Alto. The dog was given to a friend from Kentucky, in the hopes that this placement would better fit his needs.

RUBY ROUCH AND BESSIE: The Coolidges also owned two "brown" collies, Ruby Rouch and Bessie. Ruby Rouch had been left on the White House doorstep by someone who obviously felt the First Family wouldn't mind the added responsibility. The staff referred to her as "Foxy" or "Mule Ears," but never around Grace Coolidge. Bessie has been overshadowed by the many other family pets, and nothing substantial is known about her.

HERBERT HOOVER
In Office: 1929–1933

POLITICAL PARTY: REPUBLICAN

Warren Harding may have owned the first celebrity presidential dog, and Calvin Coolidge may hold the record for most dogs in the White House, but Herbert Hoover holds his own distinction. He was the first candidate for president to owe his election in large part to his dog.

When Hoover received the Republican nomination in 1928, he brought exceptional experience to the ticket. During World War I, he managed the U.S. food supply, providing food for the Allies while preventing food shortages on the home front. After the war, he earned the nickname "the Great Humanitarian" by overseeing relief efforts in war-torn Europe and Russia. He then served as secretary of commerce under President Harding and President Coolidge, during which time he oversaw a booming economy. While he was greatly respected, he had never held elected office. His campaign advisors worried that Hoover's reputation as an efficient, successful bureaucrat might also make him seem rigid or severe. They devised a public relations ploy that would be copied (usually to much less benefit) by many future office seekers—they brought his dog front and center.

King Tut was a Belgian shepherd that Hoover and his wife, Lou, had owned since 1922, when Hoover acquired the dog while on government business in Belgium. Tut loved his family and displayed all the characteristics of his breed—intelligence, loyalty, and the instinct to protect. Hoover adored him. The Hoover campaign took a photo of the candidate, smiling, posed with King Tut. Thousands of copies were printed and distributed. This charm offensive worked; King Tut and the Hoovers moved into the Executive Mansion in March 1929.

Once ensconced at 1600 Pennsylvania Avenue, King Tut would routinely fetch newspapers for President Hoover. If the weather was nice and the commander in chief wanted to read the news outside, Tut would rest upon sections of the paper Hoover had already finished, acting like a canine paperweight, preventing the wind from scattering them.

True to his breed, King Tut patrolled the perimeter of the White House at night, guarding against intruders. The Executive Mansion has always been a very busy place, with friends, family, aides, advisors, lobbyists, office seekers, security, staff, tourists, and press wandering the grounds. For a

King Tut helped Herbert Hoover win the election, but the strain of guarding the president shortened the dog's life.

dog conditioned to remain vigilant, it can be an overwhelming place to call home. King Tut grew increasingly anxious as weeks passed, and he eventually stopped sleeping and eating. He also grew increasingly aggressive toward strangers. Concerned for his dog, President Hoover sent King Tut back to his previous home, which was being rented by Congressman Frederic Walcott of Connecticut. The return home without his master did little to improve the dog's appetite, and he died in October of 1929. The First Family chose not to publicize the information, because they did not want an avalanche of dogs gifted to them by a sympathetic populace.

Upon President Hoover's election, many Americans were optimistic about the future. Years of peace and prosperity had eased the pain of the Great War, and Hoover's excellent résumé seemed a guarantee that he could handle any crisis to come. (*Also, did you see the picture of him with his dog?*) When the stock market crashed in October 1929, seven months into his administration, the country lurched toward a depression. Hoover, the man who fed a starving Europe after the war, was somehow unable to handle the crisis. Calvin Coolidge had not been enthusiastic about Hoover's becoming president. "For six years," multiple sources report Coolidge saying, "that man gave me unsolicited advice, and all of it was bad." His misgivings were borne out by Hoover's handling of what became known as the Great Depression.

Hoover's campaign decision to feature King Tut prominently proved almost as much a mirage as his résumé. While the family obviously loved dogs, the public's desire to send them pets proved problematic. Fortunately, they did eventually find dogs that fit their lifestyle, but by that point, they'd test-driven half a dozen other dogs who had to be rehomed.

No amount of dog-related publicity could have saved Hoover in the 1932 election. He was crushed by the governor of New York, a distant cousin of a

OTHER HOOVER DOGS

GILLETTE: Colonel William "Wild Bill" Donovan gave the president a Gordon setter named Gillette as an Inauguration Day present. Gillette had won prizes at the Madison Square Garden dog show, but he too appears to have been unsuited to life with the president. Gordon setters are born to run and require sixty to ninety minutes of vigorous exercise each day. They are also slow to mature. Perhaps this explains why the Hoovers gave him to the superintendent of a nearby zoo, reportedly because he "barked too much."

GLEN: A collie named Glen had been given to First Lady Lou Hoover in November of 1928 and moved from S Street (where the Hoovers resided during his time as commerce secretary) to 1600 Pennsylvania Avenue. Glen did not get along with the other Hoover dogs and left to live with the family of one of Hoover's secretaries.

PATRICK, PATRICK II, AND SHAMROCK: A series of Irish wolfhounds—all given to Lou Hoover by a former classmate, Mrs. Norwood B. Smith—spent time with the family. Patrick arrived a few weeks after the inauguration, on March 30, 1929. (Lou traded a schnauzer named Whoopie for him.) The new dog died of an infection shortly afterward. Mrs. Smith sent a replacement (known as Patrick II) in August of that year. Patrick II was described as "sensitive and shy," and bonded with the First Lady, but the timidity he former president. The new commander of chief, a patrician who had run unsuccessfully for vice president in 1920, was Franklin Delano Roosevelt.

The Hoovers had a number of other dogs, but many of them spent little time with the family.

showed around strangers eventually prompted Lou Hoover to trade him for a third dog, Shamrock. Shyness was *not* Shamrock's problem. Instead, he proved overly aggressive, and the Hoovers shipped him off after he bit one of the Marine guards at Camp Rapidan.

YUKON: A Siberian husky named Yukon arrived sometime in 1929 as a gift for the president. While the dog's behavior was not an issue, Yukon hated the summer heat of Washington, D.C. After sending him north to Canada for the summer, the Hoovers decided to give him to a friend living in a region where cool weather better suited the dog.

PAT: In May 1930, the Hoovers finally found a dog to match their tastes. Pat, a German shepherd, arrived as a gift from a supporter in Georgia. Like King Tut, Pat habitually patrolled the White House grounds, but unlike his predecessor, he enjoyed his time doing so. Pat remained with the family for the rest of President Hoover's time in office.

WEEGIE: Weegie, a Norwegian elkhound given to the family in 1931, received his name from the president's granddaughter, Peggy Ann. As a breed, Norwegian elkhounds make excellent watchdogs. Given the president's affection for King Tut and Pat, both of whom fell into the general "police dog" grouping of the day, perhaps the Hoovers valued the extra security such dogs bring. Weegie also remained with the family throughout their time in office.

6

NEW DEAL DOGS

FALA ROOSEVELT
Scottish Terrier

As the popularity of German shepherds rose in the 1920s (thanks in large part to the cinematic heroism of Rin Tin Tin), their intelligence and attentiveness brought them into wide use as working dogs. Shepherds gained increased visibility as police dogs throughout the United States, and the military began breeding and training their own canine warriors. In 1928, German shepherds took on a very different kind of job—guiding the blind.

Morris Frank (1908–1980) grew up in Nashville, Tennessee, and spent his early years guiding his blind mother. At the age of six, he lost the sight in one eye when he struck a low-hanging tree branch while horseback riding. A decade later, he lost the sight in his other eye while boxing with a friend. Frank hated how his disability hampered his independence, and he struggled to find a way to regain the freedom he remembered from his youth. When he attended Vanderbilt University, he tried paying other students to guide him, but he noticed that young, collegiate males can be surprisingly inattentive and unreliable. In November 1927, his father read him an article from *The Saturday Evening Post* detailing the use of German shepherds to assist European veterans who had been blinded by exposure to mustard gas in the Great War. Frank realized a dog could be key to regaining his independence.

The author of the article in *The Saturday Evening Post,* Dorothy Harrison Eustis, lived in Switzerland, where she bred German shepherds for use by the police. She wrote the piece for the magazine after visiting a guide dog school outside of Berlin. Just as the school had captured her attention, her article garnered widespread interest among readers. She began receiving bags of mail asking for more information, but the letter that changed the world came from twenty-year-old Morris Frank. He wrote:

Is what you say really true? If so, I want one of those dogs! And I am not alone. Thousands of blind like me abhor being dependent on others. Help me and I will help them. Train me and I will bring back my dog and show people here how a blind man can be absolutely on his own. We can then set up an instruction center in this country to give all those here who want it a chance at a new life.

Dorothy Harrison Eustis wrote an article about guide dogs for The Saturday Evening Post. *By helping train German shepherds to assist the blind, she became a pioneer of the disability rights movement.*

In February 1928, Frank traveled to Switzerland, where he trained extensively with a female German shepherd named Kiss, whom he renamed Buddy. In June of that year, he returned to the United States with Buddy leading the way. They were the first ever human/guide dog team in North America. Because the idea of a dog aiding the blind was so new, few hotels, restaurants, or modes of transport allowed guide dogs to accompany their human partners. Frank launched an intense public relations campaign, demonstrating Buddy's capabilities. He impressed reporters by crossing two of Manhattan's most dangerous streets safely, and he traveled the country demonstrating the advantages guide dogs offered the blind.

Frank and Eustis established The Seeing Eye, the nation's first guide dog school, on January 29, 1929. Initially, they operated out of Nashville, but they realized a cooler climate worked best for year-round training. The Seeing Eye eventually settled in Morristown, New Jersey, where it remains today.

Buddy traveled over 50,000 miles with Frank, proving that guide dogs offered a true sense of independence to their partners. The pair met with Presidents Calvin Coolidge and Herbert Hoover. Shortly before her death in 1938, Buddy joined Frank on a flight from Chicago to Newark, becoming the first service animal permitted in commercial air travel. Frank had five other German shepherd guides in his lifetime, all of them named Buddy.

As the Roaring Twenties collapsed into the Great Depression, millions of Americans lost their livelihoods, and charities struggled to handle the increased demand for services. The Seeing Eye, however, did not consider their clients charity cases. While no one has ever been turned away for inability to pay, the organization has charged a $150 fee for trainees to reinforce the idea that blind people are capable and do not require handouts, only accommodation. (The fee has remained unchanged since 1934.) This philosophy of assistance, not charity, fit neatly into the New Deal era of public works programs, where the federal government created jobs to boost the economy while preserving and bolstering personal pride. Just as President Roosevelt's programs offered hope to the jobless, The Seeing Eye offered it to the blind.

In 1928, Morris Frank and his German shepherd, Buddy, astonished reporters by crossing busy streets in Manhattan. Frank's desire for independence helped shift popular perceptions of the blind from tragic charity cases to capable members of the community.

Since its inception more than 90 years ago, The Seeing Eye has trained over 17,600 human-dog partnerships. According to the organization, there are nearly 1,700 active working partnerships in the United States today. There are now a dozen schools training guide dogs (only dogs from The Seeing Eye can properly be called Seeing Eye dogs), and an estimated 10,000 working partnerships exist nationwide.

The lifelong work of Morris Frank and his dogs inspired legislation in all fifty states guaranteeing service dogs entry into public spaces. The disability rights movement, which blossomed in the mid-seventies and led to the Americans with Disabilities Act in 1990, arose from the understanding that disabled people can lead full and satisfying lives if their needs are recognized by society at large. (President George H. W. Bush, who signed the Americans with Disabilities Act into law, acquired a service dog two decades later and became the first president to take advantage of the freedoms Morris Frank fought for almost a century earlier.)

In 2005, a sculpture of Morris Frank and the original Buddy was installed on the Morristown Green. The piece, created by John Seward Johnson II, depicts the team midstride, with Frank's hand raised to signal the Forward command. The monument was placed along a route the pair traveled each day on their way to and from work at The Seeing Eye. To this day, Seeing Eye students walk the same route, past this tribute to the first guide dog team in the United States.

FRANKLIN D. ROOSEVELT
In Office: 1933–1945

POLITICAL PARTY: DEMOCRATIC

While many animals have called the White House home, few if any have been as omnipresent as Fala, the Scottish terrier belonging to Franklin Delano Roosevelt, the thirty-second president of the United States. If Warren Harding's Laddie Boy represents the canine as celebrity, Fala signifies the dog as icon. In less than five years at the White House, Fala met world leaders, appeared in two MGM newsreels, inspired one of the most famous political speeches in American history, helped American soldiers identify Nazi spies, and had a cameo in an Oscar-winning romantic comedy. As historians continually rank Roosevelt as one of the greatest presidents in American history, so must we consider Fala one of the most consequential dogs the nation has produced.

President Franklin Roosevelt took his dog everywhere—even to high-level, top-secret meetings with world leaders.

Born on April 7, 1940, Fala was given to Roosevelt by his cousin Margaret "Daisy" Suckley in November of that year. The puppy—originally named Big Boy—had been trained by Daisy to sit

President Franklin D. Roosevelt owned a specially designed car that allowed him to drive despite his polio-weakened legs. He often took his beloved dog Fala along on his outings.

up, roll over, and jump. The president took an immediate liking to the dog, whom he renamed Murray, the Outlaw of Falahill, after one of the president's ancestors. That mouthful soon became simply Fala.

Scottish terriers are extremely loyal dogs, and they often serve as effective watchdogs. These characteristics proved true for Fala, who accompanied the president nearly everywhere. The constant publicity bestowed on Fala helped propel Scotties into greater popularity. The American Kennel Club estimates that Scottish terriers were the fourth most popular breed of the 1930s.

During the early 1920s, Roosevelt fell ill with what doctors diagnosed as polio (which some historians now believe may have actually been Guillain-Barré syndrome). This illness left him paralyzed for the rest of his life, although his family and aides worked diligently to conceal the extent of his disability. Custom leg braces enabled him to walk with the assistance of others, and Ford manufactured a car with specially designed hand controls so Roosevelt could continue to drive. Fala often accompanied FDR as he drove around his Hyde Park, New York, estate. While Fala had never been trained to assist Roosevelt with any medical issues, the dog's company must have eased the president's mind. The issues facing the nation were enormous and certainly weighed heavily on the commander in chief. Having Fala by his side, even for car rides around the estate, must have been comforting.

More exciting outings involved the terrier meeting world leaders. Fala joined the president for the Atlantic Charter conference in August of 1941 and met British prime minister Winston Churchill. After the United States officially entered World War II, Fala traveled with FDR on defense plant inspection trips. In 1943, he met President Manuel Ávila Camacho of Mexico. That same year, Fala accompanied the president to the highly secret First Quebec Conference, where the United States and the United Kingdom famously agreed to share nuclear technology. With these trips, Fala was present for the planning of World War II (prior to the United States' official entry into the war), as well as the early outlines for the postwar world and the dawn of the nuclear age. Pretty heady stuff, especially for someone trained to sit, roll over, and smile on command.

Even with such an extensive itinerary, Fala spent most of his time at the White House, and he probably preferred it that way. Each morning, when the president received his breakfast, FDR's tray also held a bone for his beloved Scottie. In the evening, Fala received a full dinner, but, as many presidential dogs discover, White House staffers are only too happy to feed the boss's dog throughout the day (after overindulgence made the dog ill, FDR forbade the practice). At bedtime, Fala slept on a chair at the foot of Roosevelt's bed. It was an ideal existence, receiving presidential treatment without the burdens of the actual presidency.

In 1943, Fala found his way into movie theaters. First, MGM constructed a short newsreel film called *Fala: The President's Dog*. In this bit of staged nonfiction, FDR makes the dog earn his dinner by performing tricks. The narrator pretending to speak for the president breezily utters one of cinema's strangest non sequiturs: "The more I hear of the Nazis, the more I love my dog."

An arguably more interesting cinematic experience can be found in *Princess O'Rourke,* a largely forgotten romantic comedy from that same year. In the film, a princess whose unnamed European country is currently occupied by fascist troops arrives in the United States. The exiled monarch (played by Olivia de Havilland of *Gone with the Wind* fame) pretends to be an average citizen to find relief from the pressures of royal life. In the process, she falls in love with an American pilot (Robert Cummings, who later starred in *Dial M for Murder*). The couple eventually wind up at the White House, where their pure love is almost undone by their differing circumstances. The princess is locked in the Lincoln Bedroom by her meddlesome uncle, and it looks as if the young lovers shall never be reunited. The princess writes an impassioned letter explaining everything to the president. She slips the letter under the door, where Fala retrieves it, taking it directly to FDR. The president then summons a justice of the Supreme Court (though it is the middle of the night), and the young lovers are married. Although there are conflicting reports, most sources claim the canine actor was not Fala himself, though the film shot some scenes on location in the White House. The film won an Oscar for its screenplay, but Fala (or his double) was snubbed during awards season.

In 1944, Fala accompanied President Roosevelt on a trip to the Aleutian Islands, off the coast of Alaska. The journey itself was largely unremarkable, but its aftermath impacted the 1944 presidential campaign. With the success of the D-Day invasion of mainland Europe and the steady progress of island-hopping Marines in the Pacific theater, Roosevelt's Republican opponents could not criticize his prosecution of the war. Looking for something that could damage FDR politically, some conservatives began to spread a story that Fala had been forgotten on one of the islands and that a naval destroyer had been sent to retrieve him, costing taxpayers an exorbitant amount of money and wasting time and energy for a shipload of seamen. The president, borrowing an idea offered to him directly by *Citizen Kane* auteur Orson Welles, mocked his foes during a speech to the Teamsters on September 23, 1944. He said:

> *These Republican leaders have not been content with attacks on me, or my wife, or on my sons. No, not content with that, they now include my little dog, Fala. Well, of course, I don't resent attacks, and my family don't resent attacks, but Fala does resent them. You know, Fala is Scotch, and being a Scottie, as soon as he learned that the Republican fiction writers in Congress and out had concocted a story that I'd left him behind on an Aleutian island and had sent a destroyer back to find him—at a cost to the taxpayers of two or three, or eight or twenty million dollars—his Scotch soul was furious. He has not been the same dog since. I am accustomed to hearing malicious falsehoods about myself. . . . But I think I have a right to resent, to object, to libelous statements about my dog.*

The speech, the first of Roosevelt's fourth presidential campaign, was broadcast live on every major radio network in the United States. The union

OTHER ROOSEVELT DOGS

MEGGIE: This Scottie predates Fala. When Franklin Roosevelt moved from New York to Washington, D.C., in March of 1933, the family had Meggie, a feisty terrier whose primary attachment was First Lady Eleanor. The terrier followed Mrs. Roosevelt everywhere, even attending press conferences. Her interactions with the press would prove to be her undoing. The FDR Library reports that during the president's first year in office, Meggie bit the face of Associated Press reporter Bess Furman, just as the journalist inquired about the dog's reportedly bad behavior. (Mrs. Roosevelt attempted to smooth things over by offering to write an article about the incident for the AP, but the news syndicate declined.) Meggie left the White House shortly after the incident to live with a Roosevelt family friend.

MAJOR: President Joe Biden isn't the first commander in chief with a German shepherd named Major, nor is Biden's Major the first of his name to have issues with aggression. FDR's Major, a gift from the New York State Police while Roosevelt served as governor of the Empire State, apparently had difficulty adjusting to civilian life. He terrorized the

members in the room with the president howled with laughter throughout the remarks. President Roosevelt won his 1944 reelection campaign by a comfortable margin.

Among Americans, Fala attained such a level of fame that the average citizen knew him by name. During the Battle of the Bulge (December 1944/January 1945), American troops worried about German saboteurs infiltrating their positions would ask unfamiliar soldiers "What's the name of the presi-

White House maids, bit the hand of someone reaching through the White House fence, and—like Pete, the bull terrier belonging to the president's cousin (and predecessor) Theodore Roosevelt—caused an international incident. Ramsay MacDonald, the British prime minister, must have triggered the dog's protective nature during a 1933 state visit. According to the *New York Times*, the dog nipped the visiting dignitary. In a separate incident, the *Times* reported, Major also bit Senator Hattie Caraway of Arkansas. Major, like Meggie, left 1600 Pennsylvania Avenue in December 1933.

WINKS: Shortly after the Roosevelts exiled Meggie and Major, they acquired Winks, a Llewellin setter they purchased in Warm Springs, Georgia. Winks caused considerably less trouble than the family's previous dogs. No record exists of his behaving aggressively. According to a February 27, 1934, article in the *Pittsburgh Press*, Winks's idea of mischief was consuming the entirety of a yet-to-be-served breakfast meal of bacon and eggs *for eighteen people*. Less than a year into his tenure as First Dog, Winks collided with an iron fence on the White House grounds and died of a concussion. He lies in rest at a pet cemetery in Silver Spring, Maryland.

dent's dog?" as an extra level of security. This makes him the only presidential pet used to counter espionage (that we know of).

Franklin Roosevelt died on April 12, 1945, in Warm Springs, Georgia. Fala was present when the president passed, and his response—like that of James Garfield's Veto—was out of character. In his biography *FDR's Last Year*, Jim Bishop described Fala's reaction as follows:

He had been dozing in a corner of the room. For a reason beyond understanding, he ran directly for the front screen door and knocked his head against it. The screen broke and he crawled through and ran snapping and barking up into the hills. There, Secret Service men could see him, standing alone, unmoving, on an eminence. This led to the quiet question: "Do dogs really know?"

After the president's funeral (which Fala attended, of course), the dog accompanied former First Lady Eleanor Roosevelt to her home, Val-Kill Cottage, where he lived for another seven years. Mrs. Roosevelt recalled in her autobiography, "Fala accepted me after my husband's death, but I was just someone to put up with until the master should return."

On April 5, 1952, Fala died, just two days short of his twelfth birthday. The Roosevelt family had him buried in the rose garden at Springwood, the president's Hyde Park estate. His grave sits roughly ten yards behind that of his beloved master's. Even in death, he remains at FDR's side.

HARRY S. TRUMAN
In Office: 1945–1953

POLITICAL PARTY: DEMOCRATIC

President Harry Truman reportedly said, "If you want a friend in Washington, get a dog." It's one of the most famous quotes associated with Truman, right up there with "The buck stops here." It still appears on shirts and coffee mugs, is referenced by politicians and political commentators, and is treated as conventional wisdom about the cutthroat nature of American politics. Wise though the statement may be, Truman never actually said it. The line can be traced back to the Samuel Gallu play *Give 'em Hell, Harry.* In the playlet, Gallu gives his Truman the line "If you want a friend in life, get a dog."

There were two dogs in the Truman White House, but neither lasted long. The first was Mike, an Irish setter given to the president's daughter, Margaret, shortly after Truman assumed the office in the wake of Franklin Roosevelt's death. Mike spent that summer at the family homestead in Independence, Missouri, rather than at the White House.

Harry Truman did not share his daughter Margaret's love of White House pets.

When he finally made it to Washington, Mike developed rickets, a disease causing soft and deformed bones (usually due to a calcium deficiency), and suffered additional health problems from eating the many scraps provided by the White House staff. Margaret sent Mike to live with a farmer in Virginia.

President Truman's second and more well-known dog was a cocker spaniel puppy sent by a supporter from Missouri to the president in 1947. Named Feller, the spaniel arrived in the White House only to be promptly regifted to the president's personal physician, Brigadier General Wallace Graham.

A public outcry arose, with critics calling President Truman "anti-dog" and some letter writers criticizing Dr. Graham for accepting the gift. Why it would be "pro-dog" for a puppy to remain with an owner who does not want him or for someone who does want the puppy to not take it in remains unexplained. Eventually, Dr. Graham passed Feller to a friend in an effort to remove himself from the controversy. The dog bounced from one home to another, passed between a number of different military people and bureaucrats. Feller lived at Camp David (then known as Shangri-La), traveled to Italy, and eventually settled down on a farm in Ohio.

According to author Stanley Coren, President Truman did not mince words when speaking of either pet. Coren reported that Truman referred to Feller as a "dumb dog," which seems a bit unfair, given how quickly the cocker spaniel was moved on to another home. Mike, however, stained at least one antique rug. "Do we have to stand and watch," the president allegedly fumed, "as that moron of an animal vandalizes the nation's property?" Mike, he decided, was "a damn nuisance."

Dog ownership can be hard, particularly when the canine in question is an unsolicited gift. Perhaps the family preferred the Executive Mansion to remain a pet-free home. Margaret may have dissented. After all, she went on to write *White House Pets,* a charming (if sometimes fanciful) history of animals in the Executive Mansion. In it, Margaret even mentions an animal her father didn't mind having around, at least on the balcony. The president, she remembers, often fed the local squirrels. By some accounts, at least one squirrel—nicknamed Pete—strolled the grounds with President

President Harry Truman couldn't understand why anyone would care if he gave away this adorable puppy named Feller. Is it surprising that Truman left office with exceedingly low approval ratings?

Truman. If you want a friend in Washington, President Truman might actually have said, look no further than the critters in your own backyard.

7

COLD WAR DOGS

HEIDI EISENHOWER
Weimaraner

While not every president for the first 125 years of the Republic was a dog owner, there was one animal owned by every POTUS up to this point: horses. Whether used for farming, transportation, warfare, hunting, or sport riding, horses were invaluable in early American society. It wasn't until the second decade of the twentieth century that automobiles replaced equestrian transport. By the end of World War II, as the American population became increasingly urban and car-centered, horses largely surrendered their role as working animals and became something much closer to family pets than to beasts of burden. This resulted in a significant reduction in the equine population. The Humane Society reports that the number of horses and mules dropped from a high of roughly 26.5 million in 1915 to just over 3 million by 1960.

As a result, American presidents also largely abandoned horseback riding as the decades passed. Theodore Roosevelt had once worked as a cowboy and rode often during his presidency. By the 1950s, even with a competent horseman like Dwight Eisenhower as president, the practice was far less common.

While some later presidents (notably Ronald Reagan) have enjoyed riding, the last great era of White House horses happened in the 1960s. During a period when Westerns like *Gunsmoke* dominated television and John Wayne cowboy films ruled the box office, the idea of an equestrian president certainly held wide appeal. However, the two presidents who dominated the decade, though both horse owners, represented wildly different strands of equine culture.

John F. Kennedy and his wife, Jacqueline Bouvier Kennedy, grew up in the lap of luxury. As horse-riding among the general populace fell, young Jacqueline fell in love with riding. (Her husband's notoriously bad back prevented him from riding with her.) Determined to continue riding, Mrs. Kennedy insisted that the family rent a home in northern Virginia where she could gallop around the countryside in relative privacy.

First Lady Jacqueline Kennedy rides her horse, Sardar, on the grounds of Glen Ora, the estate the Kennedys rented in Middleburg, Virginia.

Lyndon Johnson shared Mrs. Kennedy's love for horses. Born in rural Texas and self-made, he always felt like an outsider during his time as vice president. His rough-hewn, larger-than-life Texas style didn't fit in with that of the moneyed Ivy League world of the Kennedys and their inner circle. The former Senate majority leader, a man whose power had once been formidable, found himself in a largely ornamental role as JFK's understudy. The president rarely consulted him, and some of the president's closest confidants, like Attorney General Robert Kennedy, openly loathed him.

In an effort to curry favor with President Kennedy (and hopefully regain some of the power he surrendered when he left the Senate for the vice presidency), Johnson sent the Kennedy family some gifts: a small herd of Herefords and a pony for the president's daughter. This gesture, while received with smiles and warmth, did little to enhance Johnson's stature in the administration.

The pony, a three-year-old christened Tex, lived on the farm the Kennedys rented in northern Virginia. Occasionally, Tex visited the White House. However, Johnson's pony never captured the imagination the way another of Caroline's horses, Macaroni, did.

Macaroni was around ten years old when the Kennedy family moved into the White House, and he arrived with them. A misconception exists that LBJ gave Caroline this horse as well, but this is untrue. Likely, this belief simply conflates Macaroni's story with that of the lesser-known Tex. Caroline enjoyed riding, and the sight of a well-dressed little girl on her horse proved irresistible to photographers. In 1962, Caroline appeared on the cover of *Life* magazine, sitting astride Macaroni. This iconic image doubtless led many American children to beg their parents for a pet horse.

Macaroni wasn't always as adorable as he appeared. Margaret "Peggy" Foster, wife of Secret Service agent Robert Foster, recalled that Macaroni bit one of the agents responsible for protecting Caroline. There are no public reports of a rogue presidential horse attack, so any injuries incurred were undoubtedly mild. The pony was not exiled from the White House, as FDR's German shepherd Major and Teddy Roosevelt's bull terrier Pete had been. Both of those dogs had assaulted foreign dignitaries. Macaroni's only awkward action with a visiting official was decidedly milder. In 1962, he ate a bouquet of daffodils out of the hands of Empress Farah Pahlavi, the visiting wife of Iran's shah.

According to the American Horse Council, a trade organization that represents the horse industry, the current horse population of the United States is over 7 million. This creates nearly a million jobs and generates around $50 billion annually. The horse world is large and encompasses a wide array of activities, from recreational riding to dressage, from carriage horses to racehorses.

The tensions represented by the divide between the Kennedys and LBJ persist to this day. Sarah Maslin Nir, a *New York Times* journalist and the author of *Horse Crazy,* told *Smithsonian Magazine* in 2020, "Horses both symbolize our independence, as in cowboy culture, and in posh racing and show-jumping, our class lines."

Two presidents of the same political party, in the same era, with similar political programs, can own the same kind of animal and still project diametrically opposed images. As always, presidential animals provide a Rorschach test for the American people, allowing us to glimpse a perceived inner truth about our leaders. As with any such test, results may vary.

Caroline Kennedy sits astride her pony Macaroni. White House Secret Service agent Bob Foster (whose family would eventually be given JFK's dog Charlie) stands at left.

DWIGHT D. EISENHOWER

In Office: 1953–1961

POLITICAL PARTY: REPUBLICAN

General Dwight D. Eisenhower came to the White House with his historical legacy complete. As the Supreme Allied Commander during World War II, he oversaw the defeat of Nazi Germany. During his time in Europe, Ike—as the general was colloquially known—took note of various German innovations, like the autobahn. During his presidency, he helped shepherd the Interstate Highway System into existence, using German ideas as a blueprint. The German rocket scientists captured by his troops eventually formed the backbone of NASA. Is it any wonder, then, that Eisenhower should own a German dog?

President Dwight Eisenhower owned a Weimaraner—a rare breed in the United States during the 1950s.

Heidi, a Weimaraner, was given to President and Mrs. Eisenhower by the son of Postmaster General Arthur Summerfield in 1955. At the time, this breed was relatively rare in the United States, though celebrities like Dick Clark and Grace Kelly helped popularize the dogs. Weimaraners were originally bred as hunting dogs, used to track and kill bears, deer, and boars. They are known for their incredible loyalty, which can cross over into severe separation anxiety in some cases. They are keenly intelligent and very devoted to their families. As President Eisenhower and his wife, Mamie, often hosted their grandchildren at the White House, Heidi's family instincts were well served.

On January 27, 1958, President Eisenhower discussed the dog in a letter written to Summerfield:

Heidi is definitely an asset to life in the White House. She cavorts on the South Lawn at a great rate, with such important projects as chasing squirrels and investigating what might be under bushes. She is beautiful and well-behaved (occasionally she tends toward stubbornness but is then immediately apologetic about it). And she is extremely affectionate and seemingly happy. I am constantly indebted to you both for giving her to me.

In all likelihood, Heidi's torment of the squirrels at 1600 Pennsylvania Avenue was probably instinctual and not the result of Eisenhower's desire to undo the efforts of his predecessor, the squirrel-loving Harry Truman.

Eisenhower gave Heidi complete run of the White House grounds. When she wasn't chasing the local wildlife, she could be found in his office, receiving belly rubs. She proved gentle and loving with the First Family.

As with some other presidential dogs (Lincoln's Fido, Garfield's Veto, FDR's Meggie), the strain of living in the public eye eventually proved too much for Heidi. She occasionally jumped on members of the press, particu-

President Eisenhower sent his dog, Heidi, to his Gettysburg farm after a very costly accident.

larly if they attempted to photograph Mamie. She also had two accidents in the White House. The details of her first indoor soiling are unknown, but her second oops left a yellow stain on a $20,000 rug in the Diplomatic Reception Room. White House cleaning staff could not remove the unfortunate marking. The rug, worth well over six figures in today's dollars, had to be removed. The president, chagrined at this costly mishap, decided that Heidi would be better suited to life on his Gettysburg, Pennsylvania, farm.

Heidi lived out the rest of her life with the Eisenhowers on their farm, to which the president retired after his second term ended in January 1961. That year she had a litter of puppies, and with no reports of mishaps or incidents, it appears Heidi lived the rest of her life peacefully on the farm.

JOHN F. KENNEDY

In Office: 1961–1963

POLITICAL PARTY: DEMOCRATIC

Though his time in office was tragically cut short, John F. Kennedy's presidency was remarkably consequential. The youngest candidate ever elected president, Kennedy brought a new energy to Washington, filling his cabinet with widely respected intellectuals and filling the Executive Mansion with animals. Despite his severe allergies, the president wanted his two young children, Caroline and John Jr., to grow up with pets. The family had a cat, a parakeet, numerous horses, and several dogs.

The first Kennedy canine to call the White House home was Charlie, a Welsh terrier. Charlie had been given to the president's daughter, Caroline, by family member Ann Gargan shortly before the election in 1960. Though Charlie did not immediately join the family at the White House (living temporarily with the First Lady's mother in northern Virginia), he quickly became a favorite companion of the president. He would swim in the pool as the commander in

John F. Kennedy wanted his children to grow up around animals.

Charlie spent a great deal of time with the commander in chief. He often swam with President Kennedy in the White House pool.

chief did his daily laps. Kennedy asked that Charlie be present to greet him whenever Marine One, the presidential helicopter, landed on the White House lawn.

"Charlie was the number one dog," Margaret "Peggy" Foster, wife of Secret Service agent Robert Foster, recounted in an interview. "If challenged, he would have asserted himself." Apparently, the terrier was well aware of his position as the president's favorite. As was true with previous presidents, Kennedy surely needed the relief a dog can bring.

Dogs had been a key part of the Soviet space program. One month after the launch of the first man-made satellite, Sputnik, the USSR launched Sputnik 2, a hastily constructed craft containing the first living creature in space, a stray named Laika. Soviet scientists wanted to study the impact of launch on a living creature. Unfortunately, they made no plans to return the canine cosmonaut to earth, making Laika a martyr to the space race.

The Soviets had also sent two dogs into orbit—Belka and Strelka—returning them safely to earth. Strelka, the Soviet premier told Mrs. Kennedy, had recently had puppies.

"My mother told a funny story," Caroline Kennedy reminisced to the BBC in 2014. "She was sitting next to Khrushchev at a state dinner in Vienna. She ran out of things to talk about, so she asked about the dog Strelka that the Russians had shot into space. During the conversation, my mother asked about Strelka's puppies. A few months later, a puppy arrived and my father had no idea where the dog came from and couldn't believe my mother had done that."

This small white mixed breed dog arrived in Washington, D.C., bearing a Russian passport and the name Pushinka. This dog, still quite young, was the space puppy Mrs. Kennedy had asked for. Premier Khrushchev had delivered.

Cold War paranoia required that the dog be taken to Walter Reed Army Hospital and examined for listening devices and hidden bombs. When it turned out that she had neither, Pushinka (a Russian word that translates to "fluffy") made her way to the White House to join the Kennedy family's already extensive assortment of pets.

The president sent a letter of thanks to Khrushchev, along with a ship in a bottle. He noted that Pushinka's "flight from the Soviet

Strelka was one of the first two Soviet dogs to orbit the Earth and return safely. She gave birth to a litter of puppies not long after. One of her offspring ended up in the White House.

Union to the United States was not as dramatic as the flight of her mother, nevertheless it was a long voyage and she stood it well. . . . We both appreciate you remembering these matters in your busy life."

Pushinka, like the other Kennedy dogs, spent her White House years under the watchful eye of Traphes Bryant, an electrician turned pet wrangler. Bryant developed a close relationship with the pup.

Pushinka is Russian for "fluffy."

Knowing that the president believed animals should be an essential part of a child's life, Bryant set out to train the new arrival. He managed to teach her the trick of using the slide attached to the children's playhouse. By placing a peanut on the first step, Bryant coaxed the dog toward the ladder. As Pushinka ate the first treat, Bryant placed a peanut on the second step. In this way, he drew her to the top of the slide. When he placed a nut at the bottom of the slide, the dog scooted forward and slid to the bottom. Caroline and John Jr. found this trick quite exciting. After a vet advised that Pushinka not eat so many peanuts, Bryant stopped the practice, which ended the canine playground exhibitions.

Pushinka did not travel with the family as some of the other Kennedy dogs—notably Charlie—did. When the president packed his family off to Florida for the holidays, she remained at the White

House under Bryant's care. Why some dogs traveled with the Kennedys and others did not is unclear, though owners of multiple dogs may recognize that some animals are better suited to travel and more accepting of new environments than others. Pushinka was obviously not a stranger to long-distance travel, but perhaps she did not acclimate quickly to new surroundings.

A certain irritability was part of Pushinka's temperament. On first meeting young Caroline, she growled at the president's daughter, then four years of age. According to author C. David Heymann, the little girl promptly booted the dog in the posterior. When she recounted this story for her father later that day, he replied, "That's giving it to those damn Russians."

Those "damn Russians" certainly dominated Kennedy's presidency. When in October of 1962 an American spy plane photographed the construction of missile installations in Cuba, the world took a sudden lurch toward annihilation, in what became known as the Cuban Missile Crisis.

There are no specific references to Pushinka in memos or diary entries regarding the crisis. However, historian Martin Sandler believes that the back-channel correspondence (including the gift exchange) helped the world's two most powerful men step back from the brink. "In the end," he told the BBC, "that's what saved the world from nuclear destruction." Indeed, it is difficult to believe a person who sent your family a puppy is evil and deserves to perish at the foot of a mushroom cloud.

Traphes Bryant recalled President Kennedy requesting that Charlie be brought to the Oval Office at the height of the standoff. The president stroked his terrier for a few minutes and appeared to visibly relax in the process.

Charlie and Pushinka's puppies were born in the summer of 1963. Two went to family friends and two were given to children who wrote to request a dog of their own. Some of their descendants may still be out there, their owners unaware of their dogs' presidential lineage.

Finally he returned Charlie to Bryant, thanked him, and said, "It's time to make some decisions." After thirteen terrifying days, the two leaders reached a deal—Khrushchev agreed to remove the missiles from Cuba, and Kennedy pledged not to invade the island.

In the months that followed, tensions between the two nations began to subside. As the United States and USSR began to negotiate a nuclear test ban, Charlie and Pushinka provided an example of what warmer international relations could look like. The president's favorite dog impregnated the fluffy Soviet. In the summer of 1963, Pushinka gave birth to four puppies—Blackie, White Tips, Streaker, and Butterfly. Kennedy showed great interest in these "pupniks," regularly questioning Bryant about their progress. The Kennedys decided not to keep the puppies, giving two to family and friends and two to children who had written to the White House requesting puppies.

The president's assassination on November 22, 1963, forced Mrs. Kennedy to make a number of decisions, among them what to do with the family's many dogs. She and her two children moved to an apartment in New York City, where there was not room for all of the pets they had acquired during their time in the White House. Pushinka went to live with the White House gardener. Charlie was given to Secret Service agent Robert Foster, who had worked on the detail protecting Mrs. Kennedy and the children.

The Fosters lived in Bethesda, Maryland, a D.C. suburb. Charlie did well there.

"He was very, very protective of my children," Peggy Foster recalled in an interview. "I had a baby in May of 1964. You could put the baby in the yard with Charlie, and even the mailman wouldn't come in. He had a no-nonsense type of growl."

Of course, his years of roaming the White House grounds had conditioned him to ramble in the less structured, less secure world outside the presidential bubble. "One morning I got a call," Ms. Foster said. "Charlie had gotten out again." The dog had decided to park himself in the middle of the street, backing up traffic. He refused to move for anyone but Peggy Foster.

A few years later, when Agent Foster's assignment changed, the family moved to Worthington, Ohio. Their new home had no fence, and it became hard to keep him at home. "Charlie was very much a male stud," said Ms. Foster. One day she received a complaint from a neighbor, whose home the former presidential pet had been visiting. "I tried to chase him away," the neighbor

OTHER KENNEDY DOGS

SHANNON: This black-and-white cocker spaniel was given to the Kennedy family by Éamon de Valera, the president of Ireland. Shannon wore a collar adorned with gold shamrocks. Shannon is the only one of the White House dogs Mrs. Kennedy kept after her husband's assassination.

The Kennedy family dog Shannon sits in a chair in Hyannis Port, Massachusetts.

CLIPPER: Joseph Kennedy, the president's father, gave this German shepherd to Mrs. Kennedy. The First Lady took a strong liking toward the dog. On January 27, 1963, the *Washington Post* reported that she had been seen walking the dog outside the White House grounds, wearing sunglasses to help hide her identity. When, on another occasion, legendary journalist Helen Thomas asked Mrs. Kennedy what Clipper liked to eat, the First Lady replied simply, "Reporters."

First Lady Jacqueline Kennedy stands with her dog, Clipper, near the walkway outside the Oval Office.

Black Jack, a riderless horse (led by Private First Class Arthur A. Carlson), walks in the funeral procession of President John F. Kennedy as it turns onto Pennsylvania Avenue, en route from the White House to the Capitol Building. Black Jack also participated in the funerals of President Herbert Hoover (in 1964) and President Lyndon Johnson (in 1973).

WOLF: In August 1963, a priest from Dublin, Ireland, gave President Kennedy an Irish wolfhound that the family named Wolf. Unfortunately, the new dog did not get along well with the many other canines in the Kennedy family, particularly Clipper.

reported, "but he looked right at me and [relieved himself] on my patio door." Clearly, the terrier had learned something about partisan politics while at the White House.

In an effort to stay in the good graces of their neighbors, the Fosters tried to keep Charlie at home, but he grew increasingly unhappy being confined to their house. He began urinating inside, and it became obvious that he needed a better situation. Ms. Foster asked her veterinarian for help, and Charlie was soon transferred to a couple better situated to handle him. They were never told that their new best friend had once shared a swimming pool with President Kennedy.

LYNDON B. JOHNSON
In Office: 1963–1969

POLITICAL PARTY: DEMOCRATIC

Lyndon Johnson's reputation as a dog owner is as complicated as his reputation as president. Just as his time in office is a contrast between major achievements (the Civil Rights Act of 1964, the Voting Rights Act of 1965) and the disastrous quagmire of the Vietnam conflict, his deep affection for canines is undermined by a notorious photo of LBJ lifting the beagle Him by the ears. Larger than life and often uncouth, Johnson nonetheless proved himself a savvy political operator. He didn't use his pets as political props, and he didn't have to. Instead, the historical record indicates that LBJ just *really loved dogs*.

After leaving office, President Lyndon Johnson recorded an album of folksy stories entitled "Dogs Have Always Been My Friends."

Any discussion of Johnson and his dogs begins with a picture that appeared in the June 19, 1964, issue of *Life*. It ran as part of a cover story about the president's beagles, named Him and Her. The dogs were brother and sister, sired by Johnson's beagle named Beagle (a

President Lyndon B. Johnson caused a storm of protest when he lifted his beagle Him by the ears.

name that is perhaps a little on the nose) and born in the summer of 1963, while LBJ was vice president. The magazine story made the dogs famous, in large part due to the uproar over the ear-pulling photo.

Hundreds of enraged readers called, sent telegrams, and wrote letters denouncing the president's action. Johnson issued a public apology, but privately he expressed his confusion over the controversy. In West Texas, Johnson's home region, it had been common practice for hunters to pull dogs' ears prior to a hunt to make sure the dogs were "in good voice." Moreover, Johnson told reporters in off-the-record remarks, "I've been pulling Him's ears since he was a pup, and he seemed to like it."

The *Life* article's text noted: "Whether or not they agree with the president's way of showing affection, [the dogs] probably wouldn't swap places with any other dogs in the world. Not many dogs have been privileged to shoo birds off the White House lawn, get underfoot at a cabinet meeting, or mingle with dignitaries at a state ball." This is true, though it's doubtful that dogs are as awestruck by these people and places as status-conscious human beings are.

Sadly, neither Him nor Her lived the full life of your average beagle. Her died in 1964 after swallowing a stone. Him's penchant for shooing squirrels from the lawn proved fatal when he was struck by a car on the White House grounds in 1966.

Johnson was never dogless—Him had fathered a beagle named Freckles in 1965. However, it was a stray white mutt who captured LBJ's heart.

In September of 1972, Lyndon Johnson, more than three years into his retirement, recorded his reflections on growing up in Texas. The recordings were eventually pressed as a vinyl LP and released under the title *Dogs Have Always Been My Friends: Lyndon Johnson Reminisces*. "We've had many dogs through these years," he drawls, "and now we have Yuki. And I think they saved the best for the last."

Yuki arrived in the president's life on Thanksgiving Day in 1966. While traveling to the Johnson family ranch, Johnson's daughter Luci saw a stray dog at a gas station in Johnson City, Texas. When she found no owner for the lost animal, she brought him home for dinner. She named the dog Yuki—Japanese for "snow." The next year, she gave the dog to her father for his birthday. He quickly became the president's favorite.

"He is the friendliest and the smartest and the most constant in his attention of all the dogs I have known," the president recalled on *Dogs Have Always Been My Friends*. "We have always thought maybe he was with the circus, because he was so well trained." (No word could be found on whether any traveling circuses had recently passed through Johnson City.)

LBJ loved to "sing" with Yuki. The president would throw his head back and howl, and the dog would join in. This is also captured on Johnson's album of reminiscences. "Come on," he urges. "Sing for me!" The president offers a low *oooooo*. On cue, Yuki chimes in, baying as if at the moon. Laughter ensues.

Johnson certainly needed a faithful friend during those last years of his presidency. As the war in Vietnam escalated, so did protests outside the White House. Even in his own Democratic Party, Johnson was losing support. By early 1968, he announced that he would not seek the Democratic nomination for the presidency that summer.

The Republican Party nominated Richard Nixon that summer, and Johnson then invited the former vice president to the White House to discuss the war in Vietnam. Yuki, as usual, attended the meeting. Afterward, the men went outside to part ways. As Nixon boarded a helicopter, Yuki followed him. Johnson raced to the craft and retrieved his canine. Nixon later recalled the men sharing a laugh, with the Republican saying, "I said I wanted your job, not your dog!"

LBJ sings with Yuki as Ambassador David Bruce looks on.

In November 1968, Nixon finally attained the White House, sixteen years after his dog Checkers saved his political career. Johnson retired to his ranch with Yuki. His beloved dog was by his side when he died in 1973.

President Johnson shows a basket of beagle puppies to special assistant Jack Valenti's daughter, Courtenay, on January 5, 1966.

OTHER JOHNSON DOGS

FRECKLES: Freckles was fathered by the president's beagle Him and born in 1965. Originally, Freckles and her litter mate Kim were given to the president's daughter, Luci. When Luci married and moved to Texas, Kim left with her, but Freckles stayed behind, remaining with LBJ for the remainder of his term. She was given to a White House staffer when LBJ left office.

EDGAR: Upon the death of Him, Federal Bureau of Investigation director J. Edgar Hoover gave the president a beagle, which Johnson named Edgar in gratitude. (LBJ had earlier named Hoover "director for life," cementing Hoover's power. A dog seems like a reasonable trade for such career security.) Edgar retired with the Johnsons to their Texas ranch in 1969. Hoover remained a major power player in Washington until his death in 1972.

BLANCO: In late 1963, shortly after LBJ assumed office, a nine-year-old girl offered him a white collie, which he accepted. Hoping to avoid the endless gifting of dogs endured by previous presidents, Johnson announced that his acceptance was symbolic of all the dogs he had been offered, and that he would accept no more pups from supporters. Blanco appeared on White House holiday cards, but he was not always well behaved. Blanco bit Him and later bit Edgar (a wound that required stitches). Reportedly, Blanco also urinated on an Alexander Calder statue on loan from the Museum of Modern Art in New York. While the collie remained at the White House for the entirety of Johnson's time in office, the dog was given to a doctor from Kentucky when the Johnsons left Washington.

8

DOGS OF THE SEVENTIES

LIBERTY FORD + PUP
Golden Retrievers

An American child growing up in the early decades of the twenty-first century might have some difficulty understanding how dogs lived in the United States of the 1970s. Andrew Rowan and Tamara Kartal's 2018 study "Dog Population and Dog Sheltering Trends in the United States of America" provides an illuminating look at just how different American dog culture was fifty years ago. Using a variety of data, the study documents the shift from dogs as pets to dogs as family members.

Perhaps the most heartening change from the 1970s is the drastic reduction in animal shelter euthanasia. Rowan and Kartal's research indicates that 13.5 million cats and dogs were euthanized in 1973. This, they note, was around 20 percent of the U.S. pet population. Another 25 percent of dogs roamed the streets, making them vulnerable to any number of injuries—from car accidents to attack by other animals—as well as capture by local animal control authorities. They cite the Humane Society of the United States as reporting a 50 percent decline in euthanasia by 1985. By 2010, stray dog euthanasia had declined to an estimated 2.5 percent of pets.

How did this happen?

Over the last fifty years, various groups, including the Humane Society, have advocated "responsible" pet ownership. This can mean many things, of course, from purchasing a license for your pet to obeying local leash laws. What it almost always includes, however, is the spaying or neutering of dogs and cats. Efforts at education have increased dramatically in the last fifty years, even becoming a daily feature of the popular TV game show *The Price Is Right,* whose host Bob

Barker began reminding viewers to "have your pet spayed or neutered" during his sign-offs in 1982. According to Rowan and Kartal, the number of neutered dogs within the city of Los Angeles rose from less than 11 percent in 1971 to nearly 100 percent at present.

The push for responsibility also seems to have brought people closer to their dogs. A 2015 survey revealed that 95 percent of Americans view their pets as family members. The growing societal focus on animal welfare and more restrictive laws surrounding animal abuse and neglect have created an environment in which pet owners more often consider the comfort and state of mind of their pets.

While these trends are encouraging, it's important to view the actions of our parents and grandparents in the context of their times. When the Nixons and Carters kept their dogs in the White House kennels rather than in their bedrooms, they were operating within the standards of their era. Few dogs slept in the same bed as their owners (though Lyndon Johnson apparently did). Gerald Ford did not spay his golden retriever, Liberty, and few would have expected him to do so. As ever, the presidents of the 1970s offer us a snapshot of American values for a moment in time—and what a time it was.

RICHARD M. NIXON
In Office: 1969–1974

POLITICAL PARTY: REPUBLICAN

In 1952, the Republican Party drafted D-Day hero Dwight Eisenhower as their presidential nominee. They chose to balance the ticket with Richard Nixon, then a thirty-nine-year-old senator from California best known for his work with the House Un-American Activities Committee.

Louis Carrol, a young traveling salesman living in Texas, read an interview with Pat Nixon in which the VP candidate's wife mentioned that her two young daughters desperately wanted a dog. Carrol, whose cocker spaniel had just birthed a litter of puppies, hurried to Western Union, where he sent a telegram to Senator Nixon's office, offering one of his pups to the Nixon family. A week later, his family received a letter from Nixon's secretary, Rose Mary Woods, accepting the gift. In early September, a female cocker was sent to the Nixons. This would prove to be one of the most consequential gifts Nixon ever received.

There was little time for Senator Nixon to play with his new puppy. The campaign required

No American president owes more to a dog than Richard Nixon owes to Checkers.

Tricia and Julie Nixon with their dog, Checkers.

him to take a train tour of the West Coast. Meanwhile, the dog settled in with Nixon's daughters.

On September 18, 1952, while Senator and Mrs. Nixon were on their tour, journalists discovered a "secret" fund created by wealthy Nixon supporters to aid the senator's political endeavors. Speculation arose that Nixon had personally benefited from the money—a total of around $18,000—and various political commentators began to call for Nixon's removal from the GOP ticket. By September 22, the "Fund Crisis" required immediate action. Nixon asked the Republican National Committee to buy half an hour of television airtime so he could address the issue directly with the American people. The RNC complied, booking the 9:30 P.M. (Eastern time) slot for September 23.

Everything Richard Nixon had worked for teetered on the verge of collapse—his national reputation, his political career, his place on the 1952 Republican ticket. He sat on a stage in Los Angeles, his wife, Pat a few feet away, and faced the television cameras. When given the signal, he would have thirty minutes to save his career, a far-from-certain outcome. On the desk before him were a few pages of notes he had hurriedly cobbled together, key points to address and facts to include. Among the items he intended to discuss was a cocker spaniel puppy. The resulting speech, which aired live on September 23, 1952, focused mostly on the Nixon family's finances, but it is known to history as the Checkers speech, taking its name from the puppy who provided its most memorable moment. This televised address changed America—politically and culturally—forever.

Sixty million viewers tuned in to see what, exactly, Senator Nixon would say. He began by explaining his humble origins and laying bare his family's relatively modest lifestyle, describing in detail their personal loans, mortgages, and income. He explained that the fund in question was used exclusively for political and campaign purposes—travel and mailings directly related to his political activity—and that nothing had been spent on his private life. He told the audience that his wife wore a "Republican cloth coat" rather than the mink then fashionable among the wealthy. Then, in a master stroke, he mentioned the puppy.

Placing his hand on his brow, as if just remembering a small detail he's almost embarrassed to share, Nixon said:

> One other thing I probably should tell you because if we don't, they'll probably be saying this about me too, we did get something—a gift—after the election. A man down in Texas heard Pat on the radio mention the fact that our two youngsters would like to have a dog. And believe it or not, the day before we left on this campaign trip we got a message from Union Station in Baltimore saying they had a package for us. We went down to get it. You know what it was?
>
> It was a little cocker spaniel dog in a crate that he'd sent all the way from Texas. Black and white spotted. And our little girl—Tricia, the six-year-old—named it Checkers. And you know, the kids, like all kids, love the dog and I just want to say this right now, that regardless of what they say about it, we're gonna keep it.

It was a baldly sentimental moment, an inversion of Franklin Roosevelt's famous Fala speech that had been delivered exactly eight years before. No one had previously mentioned the Nixon puppy. The senator, recalling FDR's successful political jujitsu maneuver, chose to weaponize Checkers for the same purpose—to shame his opponents. That he was stealing a move from the iconic Democrat to beat back Democratic critics was a particularly clever bit of Nixonian knife-twisting. Though the moment appeared incidental, it was a calculated move, trading on all-American iconography—kids! puppies!—to humanize a candidate whose ethics had been questioned. Because of his busy campaign schedule, Nixon had barely met the dog at the time of the speech, and he got a few details wrong, including the gender. Checkers was female, but Nixon referred to her as "he." Nixon closed the speech by attacking his Democratic rivals and encouraging viewers to contact the RNC with their verdict on his guilt or innocence. His thirty minutes ran out before he could finish speaking, and he believed he had blown his only opportunity to clear his name.

In an article commemorating the speech's fiftieth anniversary, John Woestendiek describes the dejected politician exiting the building after the broadcast: "[Nixon] left the studio and slumped in the back of his car, spotting an Irish setter barking on the pavement. 'Well,' he said to Pat, 'we made a hit in the dog world, anyway.'"

As it turned out, Nixon had strongly underestimated the public response to his speech. Telegrams, letters, and phone calls began to pour into the RNC. They were 75 to 1 in favor of Nixon remaining on the ticket. The overwhelming public support pressured General Eisenhower and his advisors to retain

Nixon. The Republican Party easily won the White House that November, and they gained a slight majority in both the House and the Senate.

Checkers died in 1964, at the age of twelve. Richard Nixon, who immortalized her, failed in his 1960 presidential bid, before gaining the office in the 1968 election. Never officially a White House pet, she nevertheless retains an outsize legacy. (September 23 is now celebrated as National Dogs in Politics Day—sometimes called Checkers Day.) The speech—which Nixon always referred to as the Fund Speech—was a lesson to the candidate in the value of television as a means of circumventing a potentially hostile press. The entire incident soured Nixon's relationship with journalists, which had generally been favorable before the scandal. His belief that the press were his "enemies" only grew over time, ultimately reaching a peak with the Watergate scandal two decades later.

Richard Nixon finally reached the White House in 1969. His campaign focused on a supposed silent majority whose values and patriotism, Nixon claimed, went unheralded by the media. While the size and volume of such a constituency is debatable, Nixon seemed to be aligned with the American people when it came to dogs. Two of the three dogs the family owned while in the White House were among the American Kennel Club's list of top ten breeds for the 1970s. Poodles, America's favorite breed for the second decade in a row, were represented by Julie Nixon's Vicky, and Irish setters—like King Timahoe—came in at number six. (The family's Yorkshire terrier, Pasha, was not represented, but was no less beloved.)

President Richard Nixon plays with his Irish setter, King Timahoe,
on the White House lawn in 1969.

President Nixon playing with King Timahoe in Key Biscayne, Florida, in November 1971.

When the family arrived at the White House on January 20, 1969, they had two dogs—Vicky the poodle and Pasha the Yorkie. The president's staff, in a belated present for his fifty-sixth birthday, procured an Irish setter for the commander in chief. Nixon again borrowed from FDR by naming the puppy after his ancestral roots. The dog became King Timahoe, after the village in Ireland where one of his Irish Quaker grandfathers was buried. The dog moved into the White House kennels under the supervision of Traphes Bryant. A 1973 *New York Times* article notes that Nixon was initially shy around the puppy, quoting Bryant (who had recently retired from his position in the White House): "I'd take the King to the president and give Mr. Nixon goodies to keep in his desk for the dog. Then, I'd tell him what new things I'd taught Tim and he would put him through his paces."

Nixon's initial hesitance around King Timahoe fueled speculation that the dog disliked the president and approached him only to receive treats. This story plays on the cultural belief that animals can sense dishonesty and malevolence in humans: a dog recoiling from President Nixon underscores the shady, "Tricky Dick" caricature. Generally speaking, the trope is untrue, and in the specific case of Richard Nixon, it appears to be little more than an exaggeration. Whatever devious or deceitful traits critics claimed the thirty-seventh president exhibited during his political career, his time in the White House proves that he cared for dogs, and they responded in kind.

In his 1975 memoir, Bryant describes Nixon as someone who relaxed by watching the dogs play on the White House lawn while he ate dinner on the Truman Balcony. Bryant also recounts a time when King Timahoe, true to his breed, spotted a bird on the property and went into a full pointer stance. Nixon stood completely still, keenly observing the action for a full ten minutes before the bird flew off and the Irish setter relaxed.

Like many dogs, King Timahoe learned to shake hands with humans. A handshake (paw shake?) with the president's dog became a popular photo opportunity for guests at the Nixon White House. Had Timahoe truly feared Nixon (or had the president actually disliked him), this certainly would not have occurred.

All three Nixon dogs participated in the White House wedding of President Nixon's daughter, Tricia, on June 12, 1971. As the president and his daughter made their way to the Rose Garden for the traditional walk down the aisle, they passed King Timahoe, Vicky, and Pasha, each of whom wore specially made floral wreath collars for the event. As members of the family, they had to participate.

Richard Nixon's 1972 reelection was one of the largest landslides in American presidential history. While there were certainly many factors at play in his resounding defeat of George McGovern, Traphes Bryant believed King Timahoe played a role. The *New York Times* quotes him as saying, "I'm sure one [photograph] of the president working at his desk, with the red setter keeping him company, was worth 10,000 votes."

MORE ON NIXON'S OTHER DOGS

VICKY: Julie Nixon's poodle loved to watch the goldfish in the White House garden, and reportedly caught at least one. However, her most indelible moment came on the evening of August 8, 1974, as she curled up on the ottoman at the president's feet. The next day, Richard Nixon would officially resign the presidency, a victim of his own administration's role in the Watergate burglary, which he helped try to cover up. No president, before or since, has resigned the office. Certainly, the public disgrace weighed heavily on Nixon. At a moment when President Nixon must have felt abandoned by his political allies and the American people at large, Vicky was by his side.

PASHA: In the January 1, 1974, issue of *The Saturday Evening Post*, Julie Nixon Eisenhower published a children's story called "Pasha Passes By." The lively tale followed the family's Yorkshire terrier on an adventure around the White House grounds. The real Pasha loved playing with the other Nixon dogs. All three happily shared a heated kennel on the White House grounds.

Nixon family dogs King Timahoe, Vicky, and Pasha looking out a window of the White House.

GERALD FORD

In Office: 1974–1977

POLITICAL PARTY: REPUBLICAN

Gerald Ford was temporarily dogless when he took the presidential oath of office on August 9, 1974. The Fords had always been dog people, and they had previously owned two golden retrievers, but at the time of the inauguration, they owned no pets. While President Ford focused on the difficult task of restoring America's faith in government after the Watergate scandal and the catastrophe of the Vietnam War, his daughter, Susan, convinced White House photographer David Kennerly to help her acquire a puppy for the First Family. (Given the photogenic nature of puppies, she probably didn't have to do much convincing.)

President Gerald Ford presided over America's bicentennial celebration. His dog was, fittingly, named Liberty.

Kennerly tracked down a breeder in Michigan with a recent litter of golden retriever puppies. Hoping to conceal the newsworthy nature of his interest, Kennerly told the breeder he was purchasing the dog for a friend. As President Ford recounted in his 1979 memoir:

That was fine, the owner said, but what was the name of David's friend?

David said it was a surprise; he wanted to keep the name secret.

"We don't sell dogs that way," the owner replied. "We have to know if the dog is going to a good home."

"The couple is friendly," David said. "They're middle-aged, and they live in a white house with a big yard and a fence around it. It's a lovely place."

"Do they own or rent?" the owner asked.

David thought for a minute. "I guess you might call it public housing," he said.

As the breeder continued to press, Kennerly realized he would have to come clean. He explained his situation, and plans were made for the dog's trip to Washington, D.C.

One day shortly thereafter, Susan found her father in the Oval Office and asked him what his next dog would be. When he replied that it would be a six-month-old golden retriever, the puppy scampered into the room on cue. President Ford, overjoyed at this gift, got down on his hands and knees to play with the puppy.

The puppy had initially been named Streaker (a name Caroline Kennedy also gave to one of Pushinka's puppies in 1963), but Susan decided that Liberty was a better fit for a White House dog. The culture had certainly shifted since the Kennedy era—streaking had come to refer to running nude through

President Gerald Ford and his golden retriever, Liberty, in the Oval Office.

public spaces. In April of 1974, Robert Opel streaked across the stage at the Academy Awards, and that spring Ray Stevens's novelty song "The Streak" reached number one on the *Billboard* charts. As President Ford would eventually oversee the celebration of America's bicentennial in 1976, Liberty seemed a perfect name.

On October 9, 1974, President Ford discussed the puppy's arrival in a speech to Philadelphia Republicans:

This puppy has really taken over the White House. In fact, you may have seen some of us laughing up here during dinner. As I reached in my pocket to get a match to light my pipe, look what I pulled out of the pocket—some dog biscuits!

He told the audience how his daughter had conspired with Kennerly to procure the dog, and then added:

One of those inquisitive reporters that we have in Washington asked Susan who is going to take care of Liberty; who is going to feed her and groom her and take her out each night or every morning? And Susan did not hesitate one minute. She said, "Of course, it will be Dad." So, I have this feeling—this is one Liberty that is going to cost me some of mine. But in a very broader sense, that is the true nature of liberty. It comes with both privileges and obligations. Freedom, we all know, is seldom free.

Liberty soon achieved the minor celebrity status of most presidential pets. Fan mail arrived, and Susan Ford agreed to respond to these letters. For special friends of the Fords, an additional treat was included in the reply—a photo personally "autographed" by the dog herself. The president's personal secretary, Dorothy Downton, produced these souvenirs, pressing Liberty's paw into an ink pad and applying it to the photos. Though these were initially produced in batches limited to ten or twelve, demand for the keepsakes soon outpaced any reasonable expectation for what Downton and Liberty could produce. The White House created a rubber stamp of the dog's paw so each autograph request could be fulfilled.

Autograph requests only increased in 1975, when Liberty gave birth to a litter of puppies in the White House. A room on the Executive Mansion's third floor had been set aside for the delivery, with a special whelping box for the comfort of the mother-to-be. The Fords employed a trainer to assist them as Liberty neared her due date. Of course, even at the White House, the boss sometimes has to pitch in. In her memoir *The Times of My Life,* First Lady Betty Ford recalls an evening when the president took responsibility for the hugely pregnant dog:

> One night the trainer had to be away, and he left Liberty with us. "If she wants to go out," he said, "she'll come and lick your face."
> About three o'clock in the morning, she came and licked Jerry's [President Ford] face. Like a good daddy, he got up, pulled on a robe

and slippers, took the dog downstairs and out onto the south lawn. When they were ready to come back, Jerry rang for the elevator. But at night the elevator goes off.

Mrs. Ford reports that the president and his pregnant pup went unnoticed by Secret Service agents. Not trying to raise a ruckus or be a bother, President Ford chose another route.

Jerry decided to try the stairs. He opened the door to the stairwell, said, "Come on, Liberty," and up they climbed to the second floor, Liberty waddling from side to side, her stomach with nine puppies in it practically hanging on the ground. They got to the second floor, and the door to the hall was locked. You can get out, but you can't get back in. They went up again, to the third floor. Also locked. And there they were, a President and his dog, wandering around in a stairwell in the wee small hours of the morning, not able to get back to bed.

Eventually, the wandering leader of the free world found a Secret Service agent who turned the elevator on. Dog and master rode back to the third floor, belatedly returning to bed.

Liberty delivered her puppies on September 14, 1975. The first pup arrived at 12:30 P.M., and the ninth was born at 8:17 P.M. that evening. While Susan and the trainer cared for the newborn puppies, Betty Ford remained with Liberty through the process.

Liberty's puppies.

Of the nine puppies, the Fords decided to keep one, a female named Misty. Another was given to Leader Dogs for the Blind in Rochester Hills, Michigan. (Leader Dogs is the second-oldest guide dog school in the United States, behind only The Seeing Eye.) The remaining puppies were given by the Fords to various friends.

Ford served as president for less than three years, losing his reelection bid to Georgia governor Jimmy Carter. Upon leaving the White House, the Fords moved to Denver, taking Liberty and Misty with them. The popularity of golden retrievers grew exponentially as a result of Liberty's time in the spotlight. After her White House tenure, goldens began appearing in television shows (*Full House*) and films (the *Air Bud* series), portrayed as loyal, obedient, and intelligent members of the family. Indeed, Liberty's impact on American society extends well beyond her time in the White House.

JIMMY CARTER
In Office: 1977–1981

POLITICAL PARTY: DEMOCRATIC

The political fallout from the Watergate scandal combined with the national trauma of the Vietnam War provided an opening for Washington outsider Jimmy Carter to win the White House in November of 1976. Carter arrived at the White House on January 20, 1977, with a toothy grin and folksy mannerisms, but no dog.

Carter and his wife, Rosalynn, had three grown sons and one young daughter, Amy. When she moved into the Executive Mansion, Amy joined the fourth-grade class at Thaddeus Stevens, a public school a few blocks away. As most nine-year-olds would be, Amy was hesitant about leaving her home in Georgia for a new one several states away (and in the middle of the school year, no less). As a housewarming gift, her new teacher, Verona Meeder, gave her Grits, a mixed breed puppy (reportedly part collie and/or springer spaniel) born on the day Carter was elected president. The name came from one of the campaign

It's possible that President Jimmy Carter was more of a cat person during his time in the White House.

slogans used by Democrats during the election campaign, "Grits and Fritz in '76," a play on Carter's southern roots and the nickname of his running mate, Walter "Fritz" Mondale.

Grits lived in the White House kennels rather than with the family. Perhaps this had something to do with the family's Siamese cat, Misty Malarky Ying Yang, or perhaps it came down to presidential preference. Nonetheless, Amy reportedly loved the dog, and brought him to a sleepover she hosted in her White House tree house. The "tree house"—designed by President Carter and built by a White House carpenter—was an unattached platform five feet off the ground in the shade of a forty-foot-tall tree on the property.

Nine-year-old Amy Carter with her beloved cat, Misty Malarky Ying Yang, on January 20, 1977—the day of her father's inauguration.

The new arrival was not universally loved. According to the *New York Times*, Misty (as Amy called her cat) did not get along with Grits. In a 1979 article, the *Times* reported that the puppy's presence "upset" the Siamese cat, who had been with the family since their days in Georgia.

President Carter, while not the dog's enemy, was apparently not a big fan, either. Perhaps he felt that the dog's press overshadowed his policy proposals. When the White House did use the dog to raise awareness of the importance of heartworm treatment, Grits became aggressive as a technician drew his blood for the test. The incident may explain why the Carter administration never sought to center attention on him, as FDR or Lyndon Johnson did on their canine friends. Rosalynn Carter's press secretary Mary Hoyt recalled in a 2004 panel discussion of First Ladies' press secretaries, "I had a note from Jimmy Carter—no more photos of Grits. He was through with Grits!" Why the Carter administration preferred to keep their dog in the background is unknown. Perhaps the president, who won his office by promising change in Washington, did not want comparisons to Nixon's use of Checkers or even Ford's benign speeches about Liberty. Or perhaps President Carter was simply not a dog person.

When President Carter did make news for his animal interactions, it didn't go well. In August 1979, while fishing in a lake near his home in Plains, Georgia, Carter was accosted by a wild rabbit that swam toward his boat. The president used his paddle to splash the woodland critter, shooing it away. The White House released a photo of the incident, and the story dominated a slow news cycle. The net effect made Carter look silly, like a man intimidated by a bunny. His image took a significant hit, just as he was gearing up for reelection.

In September 1979, the Carter family returned Grits to Verona Meeder. Officially, this was done because Meeder's dog—Grits's mother—had recently died, rendering the teacher without a pet. In a gossipy aside, *Time* magazine reported: "As usual, however, there were leaks in high places. One was that Amy's pet was sent back because, after 2½ years, it still was not White House broken." (Eisenhower's Heidi and LBJ's Blanco would certainly understand.)

Like Grits's, President Carter's time in the White House was short, as voters chose Ronald Reagan (owner of a golden retriever fortuitously named Victory) to replace him in the 1980 election. Had he been able to use Grits on the campaign trail, perhaps history would be different.

President Jimmy Carter in a boat in Plains, Georgia, shooing away a swamp rabbit. Though Carter's actions were the correct response, the idea of a world leader battling a bunny became fodder for political cartoonists and late-night comedians.

9
END-OF-THE-CENTURY DOGS

LUCKY REAGAN
Bouvier des Flandres

With the fall of the Berlin Wall in 1989 and the collapse of the Soviet Union in 1991, the Cold War ground to an abrupt halt, leaving the United States, temporarily at least, the world's sole superpower. No longer facing the existential threat of nuclear war, Americans enjoyed the prosperity of the early internet boom and a rare budget surplus. Without an adversary against whom we could measure ourselves, we could instead look inward to define the soul of the nation.

Thus, Americans turned to the age-old question to figure out what kind of person their neighbor really was: *Are you a cat person or a dog person?* As dinner party icebreakers go, it's a fairly good one. By ascertaining your animal preference, the questioner can apply cultural assumptions to their understanding of you, completing a mental thumbnail sketch of your personality. *Dog people are like this; cat people are like that.* As with all such binary divisions, the results will be inexact (What about reptile-loving people? Or bird people?) and the assumptions as vague as a newspaper horoscope. Yet the question remains, and it can be applied at a wider level: Is the United States dominated by cat lovers or dog lovers?

The answer depends on how you measure. According to data compiled by the American Veterinary Medical Association in 2017 and 2018, over 48 million American households own dogs, as opposed to around 32 million cat-owning households. That certainly feels like a definitive answer, but other sources paint a different picture. Market research firm Euromonitor reported in 2014 that the actual cat population was 2 million greater than the dog population, largely due to a higher cats-per-household ratio. In 2016, the American Pet Products Association reported around 94 million pet cats in the United States, versus almost 90 million dogs. The varying numbers, compiled over a period of just a few years, probably say more about statistical methodology than anything else. What it seems safe to say is that the American cat-to-dog ratio is fairly even, especially when compared to global numbers. In India, Euromonitor found, dogs outnumbered cats by a ten-to-one margin. In Austria, cats have a three-to-one advantage.

Within the United States, the dominance of one animal or another is often linked to region. The northeastern United States is more cat-friendly; southerners are more likely to own dogs. A variety of factors are probably at play, from urbanization and population density to cultural tradition and the popularity of hunting. The particular nature of life in a given area has a direct impact on the choice of animal as well. An apartment dweller may choose cats because they do not require regular outdoor walks and they won't disturb the neighbors. A person living on several acres of rural land might prefer dogs for their companionship and their ability to alert their owners when someone else is approaching. The idea of "cat person" or "dog person" is therefore further muddied by circumstance.

The relative ratio of cats to dogs has remained fairly steady for the last several decades, according to the American Pet Products Association. There have been no drastic swings from one animal to the other, merely small fluctuations in the percentage of homes owning each animal and the average number of animals per household. The implication is clear—Americans as a whole are both cat *and* dog people, and we have been for some time.

Whereas in centuries past, animal ownership often stemmed from specific needs—dogs for hunting, cats as rodent control—the long, slow shift over time from working animals to pets seems to have stabilized American cultural perceptions about cats and dogs, with both being seen as acceptable pets. Continued education on responsible pet ownership has likely impacted individual choices as well, as people try to make decisions that will serve both them and their companion animals. In the end, individual preference for a specific species is borne out of a number of factors, rather than some innate and inexplicable personality quirk.

American presidents have largely been dog owners, with cats being wildly underrepresented. What to make of this? The cynical answer, which is not necessarily incorrect, is that dogs are easier to use for photo ops and campaign events. (Cats are equally photogenic, of course, but are generally resistant to following directions.) Or perhaps the always-on-the-go nature of political life is just better suited to dog ownership. Interestingly, the last three cat-owning presidents—Jimmy Carter, Bill Clinton, and George W. Bush—came to the White House as former governors. Maybe staying local is better for cats than splitting time between home and D.C.

RONALD REAGAN
In Office: 1981–1989

POLITICAL PARTY: REPUBLICAN

Ronald Reagan, former movie star and former governor of California, defeated cat-owning President Jimmy Carter in the 1980 presidential election. His conservative policies and much-lauded communication skills struck a chord with the American people, but by the end of his first term, it became apparent that something was missing. Even though Reagan won reelection in a historic landslide, his legacy felt incomplete to some in his inner circle. "I had talked the Reagans into a dog," Sheila Tate, First Lady Nancy Reagan's press secretary, said at a panel discussion of First Ladies' press secretaries broadcast on C-SPAN in 2004. "We had no kids, no dogs—no good pictures."

Ronald Reagan, ever image-conscious, understood the public relations value of owning a presidential dog.

From the standpoint of presidential public relations, history has proven that a dog is always good for photos, and photos sell an image. With the Reagans specifically—as the president was older and therefore particularly vulnerable to attacks on his health and stamina—a canine companion could provide tacit affirmation of presidential vigor to a concerned citizenry. On December 6, 1984, the First Lady was given a small black Bouvier des Flandres puppy by March of Dimes poster child Kristen Ellis. The six-year-old Ellis, born with spina bifida, had been traveling the country raising funds for the charity, which works to reduce infant mortality, for more than two years before meeting the Reagans. How the puppy came to be gifted is unknown.

Ms. Tate's wish had been fulfilled, but apparently no one on the White House staff bothered to research the breed in question prior to accepting the gift. While Bouviers do not begin to approach the size of James Buchanan's Newfoundland, Lara, they can easily grow to more than seventy pounds, a relatively large size by modern standards.

"[The Ellis family] had this little, black, cute thing," Tate recalled. "Little did I know it was going to grow *this big*!"

The Reagans named their puppy Lucky, after the First Lady's mother, Edith Luckett Davis. The name also reinforced the optimistic "morning in America" theme of President Reagan's reelection campaign and captured the general "proud to be an American" spirit of 1980s patriotism. This was the era when Rocky and Rambo were slugging it out with the Soviets in cinemas, and when cracks began to emerge in the communist bloc. With American democracy poised to defeat its Cold War nemesis at last (not to mention the approach of the Christmas holiday), a spirit of good cheer seemed appropriate.

Lucky, however, proved ill suited to life in the Reagan White House. As she continued to grow, her large size combined with her boisterous puppy energy

President Ronald Reagan and his lapdog Lucky aboard the Marine One helicopter.

to create an overpowering force. In one particularly telling photo, Lucky can be seen pulling President Reagan across the White House lawn as an amused Margaret Thatcher, then prime minister of the United Kingdom, looks on. While this is hardly equivalent to Franklin Roosevelt's German shepherd Major destroying Ramsay MacDonald's suit, it still fails to project the reassuring picture of control Reagan's image-conscious team coveted. This is not what Ms. Tate meant when she said the administration needed "good pictures."

There were other problems as well. Bouviers, a breed initially developed for hunting, require a good deal of space to exercise. The White House, while certainly spacious, is hardly an ideal place for a seventy-pound puppy to work out her energy. And it got worse: Word began to circulate that Lucky had been difficult to house-train. A reporter from the Associated Press called Ms. Tate to ask her if the dog had soiled a carpet at Camp David. "If I told you that," she replied, "it would be an unauthorized leak."

British prime minister Margaret Thatcher chuckles as Lucky drags President Reagan through the Rose Garden in 1985.

Of course Lucky was not the first—or the last—White House dog to urinate on government floor coverings, but because of Lucky's bathroom issues and her rapidly expanding size, the First Family decided to move Lucky to Rancho del Cielo, their California ranch, during the Thanksgiving holiday of 1985.

There are no statues to Lucky. She never appeared in a movie or on a sitcom. Her lasting legacy, instead, is the Presidential Pet Museum. Lucky's groomer, Claire McLean, kept some of the Bouvier's hair at the end of her grooming sessions. Claire's mother took these clippings and incorporated them into a painting of the Reagan dog. This portrait, McLean believed, was a historical artifact worth preserving. When she realized that no museum existed to celebrate the weirdly fascinating history of presidential animals, McLean decided to create one. For almost two decades, she collected and curated the museum, which at various points operated out of her home and Presidents Park in Williamsburg, Virginia. In 2017, McLean handed control of the museum to self-described "dog adventurer" William Helman. The portrait of Lucky remains the keystone artifact in the collection.

ANOTHER REAGAN DOG

After Lucky's exile to California, the Reagans gave dog ownership a second chance. The president acquired a Cavalier King Charles spaniel from right-wing commentator William F. Buckley Jr. This breed, being significantly smaller than Bouviers, did not require a wide-open ranch and would not drag the leader of the free world across the lawn. President Reagan gave the puppy, Rex, to the First Lady for Christmas in 1985. Rex remained with the First Family for the remainder of their time in Washington, then moved with them to Los Angeles in 1989.

First Lady Nancy Reagan and Rex, a gift from National Review founder William F. Buckley Jr.

GEORGE H. W. BUSH
In Office: 1989–1993

POLITICAL PARTY: REPUBLICAN

When Vice President George Herbert Walker Bush transitioned to the presidency in 1989, he brought with him years of foreign policy experience, a confident and passionate First Lady in his wife, Barbara, and an English springer spaniel named Millie. As president, Bush oversaw the first Persian Gulf war and the collapse of America's superpower foe, the Soviet Union. He signed the Americans with Disabilities Act into law and tightened restrictions on air pollution. And in the end, a book "written" by his dog Millie (as dictated to the First Lady) sold more copies than his own memoir.

Given Millie's widespread popularity, there's no shame in that.

Her first major media attention came shortly after her move to the White House. Less than two months into Bush's single term, Millie gave birth to a litter of six puppies, five female and one male. At a photo op on March 29, 1989, First Lady Barbara Bush told reporters that she'd received hundreds of

President George H. W. Bush is the only president known to have showered with his dog.

letters asking for a puppy. They kept one of the puppies, naming him Ranger. (Another of Millie's litter went to live with George W. Bush, the president's son and a future president himself. This pup, named Spot Fetcher, holds the distinction of being the only animal to live in the White House during non-consecutive terms.)

During the puppy-related flurry of publicity, Mrs. Bush shared an odd tidbit about Millie's bathing habits. The dog was too short to shower alone, she noted at the time, "But someone—a very high public official elected to office—takes a shower with Millie every week or so." The public is usually not privy to information about any president's shower partners, so the story is impossible to verify, but this particular arrangement of owner-pet bonding is likely unique in the history of presidential pets.

In July of 1989, *Washingtonian* magazine named Millie "the ugliest dog in Washington," an odd cheap shot the dog had done nothing to deserve. The text of the article, written by John Sansing, referred to Millie as the "Best Ugly Dog" and noted, "The First Lady loves her and [Millie]'s a wonderful mother." However, the kicker reads: "She hasn't bitten the president during their showers together. But let's face it. This is a very homely springer spaniel."

President Bush responded with more grace than the situation deserved, saying, "Imagine picking on a guy's dog." Eventually *Washingtonian* editor Jack Limpert apologized and sent dog treats to the White House. President Bush responded, "Not to worry! Millie, you see, likes publicity. Arf, arf for the dog biscuits."

If Millie loved publicity, she certainly must have enjoyed her time at the White House. The spaniel appeared as a character on two different TV sitcoms—*Wings* and *Murphy Brown*. After President Bush left office, he, Barbara, and the dog were even spoofed on an episode of *The Simpsons*. All of this attention paled next to what happened when Millie published her first (and, sadly, only) book.

President George H. W. Bush with his English springer spaniel, Millie, and her puppies on the White House South Lawn. One of the puppies, Spotty, became George W. Bush's pet and returned to the White House in 2001.

ANOTHER BUSH DOG

Ranger was the one spaniel puppy (of the six) the president kept from Millie's litter. He lived a relatively anonymous life in the White House, protected from the spotlight by his mother. His most lasting historical legacy is a memo from President Bush to all White House staff forbidding them to feed the puppy, who was gaining weight at an alarming rate. (Apparently, the president was not the careful literary image maker the First Lady had been.)

George H. W. Bush enjoys a walk with Millie and Ranger at Camp David in 1991.

Millie's Book, published in 1990, was supposedly written by the First Dog herself, "as dictated to Barbara Bush." It chronicled life in the White House, canine motherhood, and even the "ugliest dog" scandal. The First Lady aimed this lighthearted book firmly at children, and after-tax proceeds went to her literacy foundation. The book was a runaway bestseller, netting over $1.1 million in royalties during its first year of publication, but Millie was content to stay at home with the First Lady. She did not do a book tour.

Barbara Bush, Millie's erstwhile stenographer, was by all accounts a devoted dog owner. Anna Perez, her press secretary, recalled during the 2004 press secretaries' panel discussion at the George Bush Presidential Library that it was easy to stay on the First Lady's good side: "Don't mess with her man. Don't mess with her kids. And don't mess with her dog."

Barbara Bush, laughing, added, "But let the dog mess with you."

President Bush attempted to invoke the Fala speech during the 1992 presidential campaign when he said, referring to Democratic rivals Governor Bill Clinton and Senator Al Gore, "My dog Millie knows more about foreign policy than those two bozos." This time, referencing the family dog *didn't* work, and Bush lost his bid for a second term. Millie lived until 1997, dying of pneumonia at age twelve. She never wrote a sequel to her bestseller, disappointing many readers.

<u>IMPORTANT ANNOUNCEMENT</u>

February 6, 1992

<u>THIS IS AN ALL POINTS BULLETIN FROM THE PRESIDENT</u> *GB/*

<u>SUBJECT:</u> MY DOG "RANGER"

Recently Ranger was put on a weight reduction program. Either that program succeeds or we enter Ranger in the Houston Fat Stock Show as a Prime Hereford.

All offices Should take a formal 'pledge' that reads as follows:

"WE AGREE NOT TO FEED RANGER.WE WILL NOT GIVE HIM BISCUITS.WE WILL NOT GIVE HIM FOOD OF ANY KIND"

In addition Ranger's "access" is hereby restricted. He has been told not to wander the corridors without an escort. This applies to the East and West Wings, to the Residence from the 3rd floor to the very, very bottom basement.

Although Ranger will still be permitted to roam at Camp David, the Camp David staff including Marines, Naval Personnel, All Civilians and Kids are specifically instructed to 'rat' on anyone seen feeding Ranger.

Ranger has been asked to wear a "<u>Do not feed me</u>" badge in addition to his ID.

I will, of course, report on Ranger's fight against obesity. Right now he looks like a blimp, a nice friendly appealing blimp, but a blimp.

We need Your Help- All hands, please, help.

═══ FROM THE PRESIDENT ═══

President Bush's infamous "Ranger Memo."

BILL CLINTON
In Office: 1993–2001

POLITICAL PARTY: DEMOCRATIC

William Jefferson "Bill" Clinton won the White House in 1992, and his family moved from the Arkansas governor's mansion to 1600 Pennsylvania Avenue on January 20, 1993. President Clinton, First Lady Hillary Rodham Clinton, and their daughter, Chelsea, were not dog owners. Instead, they had a tuxedo cat named Socks. The Clintons adopted the stray Socks in 1991, after Chelsea spotted the cat playing at the home of her music teacher. Following more than a decade of canine hegemony in the White House, a feline took control of the bully pulpit.

Like many pet owners, President Bill Clinton found it difficult to mediate between his cat and his dog.

For most of President Clinton's time in office, Socks was the only pet living with the First Family. The media spotlight was intense, but he didn't seem to mind. He remained unfazed by press photographers, who lured him closer with catnip shortly after the 1992 election. (The Clintons, alarmed that a cameraman had picked up their pet during the incident, warned photographers not to do so again.) Over the course of two terms in office, he was the subject of numerous political cartoons, had a Muppet version of himself interviewed on CNN's popular *Larry King Live* (during an April Fools' Day episode guest-hosted by Kermit the Frog), and starred in an unreleased Super Nintendo video game called *Socks the Cat Rocks the Hill*. The Clinton administration used Socks as an animated guide to the official kids' White House website. He even had his own mini-scandal, as Republican representative Dan Burton criticized the White House for using taxpayer money to pay for letters written in response to children who had sent the First Feline fan mail. (Perhaps no one had told Burton about the "paw-tographs" the Ford administration sent out on behalf of Liberty?) Clearly, as all of this attention indicates, the cat was a superstar.

And then, after four full years as the foremost animal in the United States, Socks's supremacy was tested when the Clinton family acquired a chocolate Labrador retriever named Buddy.

With daughter Chelsea preparing for college, First Lady Hillary Clinton wanted to give the president a dog to help fill their soon-to-be-empty nest. The dog was donated to the First Family by Linda and Richard Renfro, owners of the Wild Goose Kennels in Federalsburg, Maryland. A puppy, temporarily named Teddy for famed animal lover and former President Theodore Roosevelt, arrived at the White House. More than 5,000 letters poured in suggesting a permanent name for the dog before the family finally settled on Buddy, in honor of the president's recently deceased great-uncle, Henry Oren "Buddy" Grisham, who had been both a mentor to the president and a dog trainer for five decades.

As pet lovers who have expanded their animal families can certainly attest, there is always a period of adjustment between established family pets and an incoming addition. First Lady Hillary Clinton's press secretary Lisa Caputo recalled, in C-SPAN's 2004 press secretaries panel discussion, being asked by a reporter how Socks was handling Buddy's arrival. "No sooner had I taken the question," she noted, "than there was an impromptu incident where Socks took a swipe at Buddy on the South Lawn. The story had gotten away from me. . . . Socks and Buddy were at odds and had to be taken to separate quarters."

President Clinton later joked that he'd had an easier time running negotiations between the Israelis and the Palestinians than he'd had trying to make peace between his two animals. Shortly before the end of the Clinton administration, the *New York Times* reported senior officials stating that Socks was notorious for hissing at Buddy.

Socks is the most famous cat to call the White House home, largely due to his friendly relationship with the press.

The First Family worked to keep peace around the White House, and Mrs. Clinton, like Barbara Bush before her, chose to capitalize on her pets' popularity by writing a children's book: *Dear Socks, Dear Buddy: Kids' Letters to the First Pets*. The book featured dozens of letters written to the Clinton animals, as well as photographs of pet life in the White House. Proceeds went to the National Park Foundation.

As the Clinton era came to a close along with the millennium, the First Family began preparations for a variety of changes. The First Lady won a Senate seat from New York in November of 2000, meaning she would remain in Washington for a significant portion of the year. Chelsea attended classes at Stanford. The president, who had recently survived impeachment, planned to retire to the family's official home in Chappaqua, New York. Eventually, the family decided to move Buddy to their New York property and give Socks to the president's personal secretary, Betty Currie, with whom the cat had developed a close friendship during his time in the White House.

Although Labrador retrievers have been among the most popular dogs in the United States for decades, only President Clinton has ever owned one while in office. Buddy arrived at the White House in 1997.

On January 2, 2002, less than a full year after President Clinton left office, Buddy was killed in an auto accident while the Clintons were away from Chappaqua. The Labrador gave friendly chase to a departing contractor and was struck by another vehicle before the Secret Service agents on the scene could retrieve him.

Socks lived with Ms. Currie and her family in Hollywood, Maryland, until 2009, when he developed cancer and passed away. While his exact age was unknown, he was close to twenty years old. Socks's legacy as the most famous cat to reside at 1600 Pennsylvania Avenue will certainly live on.

10
NEW MILLENNIUM DOGS

BO + SUNNY OBAMA
Portuguese Water Dogs

Whenever young children have called the White House home—from Tad Lincoln to Teddy Roosevelt's brood to the Kennedy family to the Obama children—animals have often accompanied. Photographs of First Families and their pets have always appeared in newspapers worldwide, and, in more recent years, are all over the internet, too, entering millions of homes and inspiring many kids to ask their parents for a furry (or feathered or scaled) friend of their own. Of course, what is less obvious to these children (although clear to their guardians) is the behind-the-scenes staff who care for those animals when the family is busy.

Kids have always wanted pet animals, and parents—aware of their offspring's maturity-related shortcomings—usually find themselves either refusing such requests or providing the bulk of a new pet's care. After all, pet ownership is more about responsibility than play. When it's pouring rain and the puppy needs a walk, somebody has to put on galoshes and head outside, and it's probably not your six-year-old. Nor can Junior spring for the vet bills or the organic duck-and-sweet-potato dog food that for some reason is all Rover will eat. Yes, many of us find that the relationships we build with our companion animals more than make up for the rainy walks and the overpriced kibble, but explaining the complexity of human-animal codependence to a child still trying to understand subtraction can be difficult.

The technology that upended the world at the turn of the century offered a solution: virtual pets.

In 1996, Japanese toy company Bandai introduced Tamagotchi to the world. A small, egg-shaped toy with an LCD screen, Tamagotchi was a digital alien

In the 1990s, Tamagotchi was briefly the coolest toy on the market.

creature that children could raise on their own. The virtual beast hatched from an egg and—given sufficient nurturing by button-pushing owners—progressed through several life cycles. Like real pets, Tamagotchi required attention. Children had to feed it, clean up its droppings, and give it regular attention. If they failed to provide the required care, their companion alien would get sick and die.

For a brief period in the late 1990s, virtual pets were omnipresent. Bandai followed the success of Tamagotchi (which they had marketed primarily for girls) with Digimon, a digital monster that could level up and battle other users' pet monsters. Tiger Electronics introduced Giga Pets, and Nintendo adapted their Pokémon franchise for the virtual pet market, allowing users to feed Pikachu by earning "watts" through real-life exercise via a built-in pedometer. The toys were so sought-after that the *Wall Street Journal* reported on a 1997 delivery made to FAO Schwarz via a Brink's armored truck.

Finally, parents could provide their children with a pet who would not require adult intervention! Kids could learn valuable lessons about the importance of caring for animals without the dire consequences of soiled rugs, emergency vet bills, and criminal charges of neglect. With prices as low as $9.99, virtual pets also cost significantly less than the real thing. Some parents were thrilled to find an economical, clean pet alternative.

Not everyone loved the virtual pet craze. Many schools—citing the constant chirping of needy pets as a distraction—banned the toys. Tamagotchi distraction also afflicted some adults. A woman in Japan crashed her car while reaching into her back seat to retrieve the beeping gizmo. And, inevitably, some children grew inordinately attached to their digital creatures, resulting in real-life Tamagotchi burials (though the toy could be reset after a pet's death).

In time, as the processing power and graphics capabilities of handheld devices improved, the idea of virtual pet ownership shifted as well. Entire games were developed around pet ownership. In 2005, Nintendo released a series of real-time pet simulation games called Nintendogs for their Nintendo DS platform. The game allowed players to adopt a "starter" dog, which they could name and call using the DS's built-in microphones. Regular animal care, such as feeding and grooming, was required, but unlike earlier pet simulators, your Nintendog could never die from neglect. Rather, the animal's friendship with the player/owner decreased.

In 2017, Electronic Arts (EA) and Maxis released an expansion pack for their bestselling game *The Sims 4*. Entitled *Cats and Dogs,* the expansion brought pet ownership into the series' fourth major entry and allowed players to interact with their pets while juggling all of the routine realities of Sim life (such as work, cleaning, and parenthood). While players could not control the animal directly, they could teach their pet tricks and provide it with toys. Once again, your pet could perish from neglect or (hopefully) old age, leaving behind a tombstone. To help combat real-world neglect, EA and Maxis donated $20,000 to the Society for the Prevention of Cruelty to Animals as part of the game's launch.

Two decades into the twenty-first century, the idea of the virtual pet is alive and well. The virtual pet craze provides a foundation for understanding the stunning popularity of President George W. Bush's *Barney Cam* internet videos and, later, the proliferation of President Barack Obama's Portuguese water dogs across social media. The presidents of this era learned how to capitalize on the proven marketing potential of presidential pets by harnessing the power of the internet, giving millions of Americans unprecedented virtual access to the White House's animal antics.

GEORGE W. BUSH
In Office: 2001–2009

POLITICAL PARTY: REPUBLICAN

In the waning days of 2002, hundreds of thousands of Americans sat in front of their hulking desktop computers, patiently waiting for their dial-up internet connection to download a four-and-a-half-minute video clip of a Scottish terrier chasing an ornament through several festively decorated rooms. That Scottie belonged to President George W. Bush, and the video was called *Barney Cam*. The star of the show, of course, was Barney, the First Dog, whose annual holiday videos dominated the web in the pre-YouTube, pre-TikTok era.

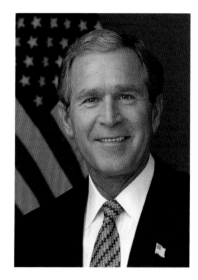

The eight-year presidency of George W. Bush was dominated by crises—the terror attacks of September 11, 2001; anthrax-dosed mail; the wars in Afghanistan and Iraq; Hurricane Katrina; the financial collapse of 2008—so perhaps it's unsurprising that the president's dog rose to prominence on the internet. Barney became a symbolic emotional support animal for a confused and anxious populace.

President George W. Bush dealt with terrorism, war, Hurricane Katrina, and financial collapse. He certainly needed the respite dogs offer their human companions.

Barney Cam *made President George W. Bush's Scottish terrier a star.*

He arrived at the White House as a puppy, a Christmas gift from president-elect Bush to his wife, Laura, in 2000. His presence at 1600 Pennsylvania Avenue was, of course, noted and captured by photographers for the usual presidential dog stories. All of this was pushed aside by the horrific attacks on the World Trade Center and the Pentagon on September 11. The seemingly frivolous nature of media attention for a pet in the aftermath of world-changing catastrophe relegated Barney's antics to the periphery. But as time passed, Americans began to crave escapism, and that's where a White House communications staffer named Jimmy Orr accidentally struck online gold.

In September of 2002, with the White House temporarily closed to the public over terrorism fears, the Bush administration's media team created a series of nine video tours of various rooms in the Executive Mansion, each led by a different administration heavyweight, including the president showing off the Oval Office.

"We got a ton of media exposure," Orr recalled in an interview. When it came time to prepare a similar video showing off the White House Christmas decorations a few months later, Orr and his colleague Jane Cook took inspiration from that year's theme, *All Creatures Great and Small*. "We came up with the idea of putting a camera on Barney's head and letting him run through the White House," Orr said. "We were just laughing! And then we had to pitch it [to the communications team]."

Every morning at eight thirty, the Bush communications team met to discuss their daily agenda, taking turns speaking about their plans. When Orr spoke, he mentioned the idea of equipping the president's dog with a tiny

First Lady Laura Bush poses with Barney and Miss Beazley next to the White House Christmas tree.

camera and chasing him through the White House. "The entire room went completely silent, and it was awkward and painful," Orr said. "I'm thinking to myself, *I am a complete moron*. Then out of nowhere . . . [the president's press secretary] Ari Fleischer says, 'That is *awesome*!'" Praise from the team soon replaced the silence.

Within the hour, First Lady Laura Bush was promoting the as-yet-unproduced video on CNN. She planned to premiere the clip at Children's National Medical Center in two weeks. *Holy shit,* Orr recalls thinking, *how do we do this?* His amusing brainstorm now had a deadline.

Orr brought in Bob DeServi, a White House communications staffer who routinely managed sets and lighting for the president. DeServi acquired a lipstick camera (a small portable recording device) and attached it to a dog collar. This plan might have worked if Barney had ever worn a collar, but living under the ever-vigilant eye of the Secret Service had allowed him to go without one. The dog howled and rolled on the ground until Dale Haney, who has handled presidential dogs since the Nixon days, advised Orr to find another plan lest the president conclude Orr was torturing the terrier, whom the president considered "the son I never had." Instead, Orr notes, they opted to follow Barney through the White House with a camera, walking on their knees to approximate a dog's-eye view of the decorations.

When Mrs. Bush debuted the finished product, titled *Barney Cam,* at Children's National Medical Center, it ran live on several major news networks. Orr recalls hearing one broadcaster murmur in disbelief, "I can't believe we're airing this." Orr couldn't believe it, either.

Barney Cam became the most popular item on the White House website, and spawned six sequels. After the first clip's wide success, members of the Bush administration began clambering for small parts in the sequel. When it came time for *Barney Cam II: Barney Reloaded,* even President Bush found room in his schedule to film a cameo, and he lectures Barney on the merits of hard work. The *New York Times* reviewed the second short film, noting, "The plot of the video is more complex than last year's video, which had no plot." It was another massive hit.

Orr left after the second film, heading to California to work with another star, Arnold Schwarzenegger, who had just been elected governor. David Almacy took his place on the Bush communications team, but he had to go through a very unusual interview process before being allowed to take over the *Barney Cam* series.

"You have to go meet Barney," he was told by Jeanie Mamo, the director of media affairs. "He's known for being a little temperamental, and if he doesn't like you, it's just not going to work." Like many A-list stars before him, Barney required approval of any director he worked with.

Almacy was taken to the Rose Garden, where he found Barney and Dale Haney. Barney was playing with a dog toy. Haney encouraged Almacy to introduce himself to the dog.

Barney and Miss Beazley follow President George W. Bush along the West Wing Colonnade on the way back to the Oval Office at the White House.

"Hi, Barney," he said. The dog looked at him, then rolled on his back. Almacy rubbed his belly. "My name's David and I'm taking over *Barney Cam* for your friend Jimmy. We're going to have so much fun making this video, and kids are going to love it." Barney popped up on all fours. Almacy glanced back at Haney and Mamo.

"Put your hand out, palm up," Haney instructed. Almacy did so. Barney licked his fingers. "Okay," said Haney. "We're good."

The video series continued for the rest of President Bush's time in office, totaling seven in all.

Mamo's comments on Barney's temperament were not unique. Speaking on the *Today* show in 2013, President Bush's daughter Jenna Bush Hager (no relation to the author) called Barney "a real jerk." She explained, "I feel bad saying that, but he didn't like strangers."

According to Almacy, Barney—whose videos became a holiday tradition—almost undermined another annual festivity. One year, while Dale Haney was on vacation, Barney got loose and attacked a turkey brought to the White House to be symbolically pardoned by the president. "The president was sitting at his desk in the Oval Office and hears what can best be described as 'a kerfuffle' in the Rose Garden," he told me. "And when he turns around, he sees that Barney and a turkey are tussling, and Barney has the turkey's neck in his mouth. The president leapt from his chair and ran out and separated them." The turkey was fine and able to be pardoned. One could argue that President Bush actually saved the bird from execution not once, but twice.

In the waning days of the Bush era, shortly after the 2008 election of Barack Obama, Barney nipped the finger of Reuters reporter Jon Decker, breaking skin. The incident was captured on video and posted to YouTube. Sally McDonough, press secretary for the First Lady, quipped, "I think it was his way of saying he was done with the paparazzi."

Whatever trouble the dog might have caused, there is absolutely no doubt that the president loved him dearly. Once, while filming a *Barney Cam* video, Almacy searched desperately for the dog, whom he needed for some cutaway shots. He found him with the president on the lawn playing fetch. "He was just like any other guy with his dog, at the end of the day, trying to de-stress a little bit." Almacy continued, "There's a whole therapeutic part of what it means to be a pet owner, and the special relationship we have with our pets."

The therapeutic benefit of animals extends beyond the pet/owner relationship as well. As frivolous as a dog-themed Christmas video might seem as an abstract idea, in the right context, it wields incredible power. Each year, Mrs. Bush debuted *Barney Cam* at Children's National Medical Center, always to joyful enthusiasm from the young audience members. "I was in tears," Almacy said. "I was talking to a lot of the parents and the doctors, and they told me that the beauty of the video is that [the kids] forget about what they're dealing with for a short time. I still get emotional just thinking about it."

In 2018, *National Geographic* reported that there are over 50,000 trained and certified therapy dogs in the United States, helping people suffering from dementia, cancer, post-traumatic stress disorder, and other ailments. The dogs improve the lives of their companions, and happily, research indicates that the pups themselves aren't stressed out by their jobs but often seem to enjoy the work.

"Everybody has a load to carry in life," Ari Fleischer, who served as President Bush's press secretary, stated. "Everybody has pressures. The president happens to have more, but no matter who you are, no matter what you do, coming home to a dog is just such a joyous, uplifting moment."

OTHER BUSH DOGS

SPOT FETCHER: An English springer spaniel, Spotty (as she was more commonly known) was named for Scott Fletcher, who played baseball for the Texas Rangers. (Prior to being president, Bush had been a part owner of the team.)

MISS BEAZLEY: Another Scottish terrier joined the Bush family as a Christmas gift from the president to the First Lady in 2004. Miss Beazley, a blood relative to Barney, soon became the more famous terrier's close companion. Though a "sibling rivalry" formed the plot of *Barney Cam: A Very Beazley Christmas*, by all accounts the two greatly enjoyed each other's company. Upon her passing in 2014, President Bush remarked, "Even though he got all the attention, she never held a grudge against him."

BARACK OBAMA
In Office: 2009–2017

On November 4, 2008, Illinois senator Barack Obama stepped onto a stage in Chicago's Grant Park to address a large and jubilant crowd of supporters.

Barack Obama promised his daughters a puppy during his 2008 presidential campaign.

He had just been declared the president-elect, and his opponent, Arizona senator John McCain, had finished a graceful concession speech moments before. The country was entering the worst financial crisis since the Great Depression and wars in Iraq and Afghanistan were raging, so there were certainly challenges ahead of him. Obama, who had routinely promised hope during his campaign, took a moment during his victory speech to address his daughters, Sasha and Malia, regarding a more specific and personal campaign promise. Acknowledging the strain a presidential campaign can place on a family and the difficulty of uprooting young lives in a move to the White House, he said, "I love you both more than you can imagine. You have earned the puppy that is coming with us!"

The Obama girls, and much of the pet-loving citizenry, were ecstatic, but there was a catch. Malia, age ten at the time of her father's election, suffered from allergies. While allergists assert that there is no breed of dog that would qualify as truly hypoallergenic, some types of dogs, like poodles or certain terriers, are less likely to provoke strong reactions in allergy sufferers. In the end, the First Family decided to get a Portuguese water dog.

Bo arrived in the White House in April of 2009, some three months after the Obamas. Massachusetts senator Ted Kennedy, the brother of President

Obama family pets Bo, left, and Sunny sit at a table in the State Dining Room of the White House, February 10, 2014. The table settings would be used at the State Dinner for President François Hollande of France.

Bo Obama, the first Portuguese water dog to live in the White House.

John F. Kennedy, gave the dog to the First Family. Kennedy loved Portuguese water dogs, bringing one of his own pets, Splash, to work with him every day. "He's not allowed to go on the Senate floor," Kennedy told CBS in 2006. "He's troubled by that. . . . He says that he behaves a lot better than most senators." The gift of Bo thus connected President Obama to the optimistic Kennedy era of the early 1960s, a torch passed to a new generation.

According to Dana Lewis, a former personal aide to First Lady Michelle Obama, the furry black dog with white "socks" coloration on his paws took his name not from the president's initials, but in tribute to the First Lady's late father, Fraser Robinson III, whose nickname was "Diddley" after legendary bluesman and rock 'n' roll pioneer Bo Diddley. The dog fit in with the First Family from the beginning, Lewis recalled. "He knew he was an Obama. He could always turn it on in public."

At Bo's birthday celebration, his brother Cappy sneaks a treat from a table in the Rose Garden. Cappy belonged to Massachusetts senator Edward Kennedy.

While the president often struggled to gain concessions from congressional Republicans, particularly after the 2010 midterm elections shifted control of the legislative branch to the GOP, Bo had no such difficulties achieving *his* priorities. According to Lewis, he found plenty of White House staffers willing to give him treats on a regular basis.

"Bo didn't fall off a truck," she said. "He was smart." The young dog learned to "knock" on Lewis's office door by butting his head twice against the door. Once inside, he received a treat and took a nap at Lewis's feet while she worked. After resting, he would leave in search of more treats. Bo learned to use the elevator near Lewis's office, pushing the button to summon it. When the doors opened, the dog would step inside and sit next to the tuxedoed elevator operator, then head out for more goodies.

In his 2020 memoir, *A Promised Land,* President Obama described similar memories of Bo's affectionate nature:

> *[Bo] gave me an added excuse to put off my evening paperwork and join my family on meandering after-dinner walks around the South Lawn. It was during those moments—with the light fading into streaks of purple and gold, Michelle smiling and squeezing my hand as Bo bounded in and out of the bushes with the girls giving chase—that I felt normal and whole and as lucky as any man has a right to expect.*

If you remove the reference to the South Lawn of the White House, Obama's reflections could be those of millions of dog lovers around the world, climbing out from under a crushing workload to enjoy the company of family.

Bo received obedience training, as many family pets do. Lewis notes that he also trained to be a comfort animal for visits to veterans and children's hospitals.

Indeed, Bo went with Mrs. Obama on visits to Children's National Medical Center and Walter Reed National Military Medical Center. The president, it turns out, wasn't the only person to whom Bo brought some modicum of peace.

Lewis recalled one specific incident where a visitor to the White House's annual Easter egg roll asked if her daughter, who was very ill, could meet the First Dog. The family was invited into the Diplomatic Reception Room. The young girl got out of her wheelchair and sat on the floor. When Bo entered, he sat with the child as she stroked him. "It's like he knew exactly what she

First Lady Michelle Obama reads "'Twas the Night Before Christmas" during a Christmas holiday program with children, parents, and staff at Children's National Medical Center in Washington, D.C., on December 12, 2011. Participants included nineteen-year-old patient Ashley Riemer, right; Bo, the Obama family dog; and Santa Claus.

needed," Lewis said. Watching Bo comfort children and veterans was, she says, "priceless."

The Obamas celebrated Bo's first birthday with a party, attended by some of his canine friends. Lewis, who served on then-senator Obama's advance team during 2008, found herself tasked with arranging the details. She worked with executive pastry chef Bill Yosses, who created an oatmeal and veal stock birthday cake. According to Yosses, "Bo, as a polite dog, waited to be invited. Not Senator [Edward] Kennedy's dog! He got one whiff of the veal stock and jumped on the table [and] began to devour it!" The party, Yosses recalled, was a "doggie success." The dogs wore party hats, just like their human counterparts (at least until they managed to dislodge them).

Bo loved canine company, and the Obamas decided to get him a permanent playmate, adding a female Portuguese water dog named Sunny in August 2013. In a statement released at the time, Mrs. Obama called the one-year-old puppy "the perfect little sister for Bo." The two were soon photographed frolicking on the White House grounds.

Of course, the massive media attention lavished on presidential pets is not without its drawbacks. In 2016, the Secret Service apprehended a man claiming to be Jesus who had driven all the way from North Dakota in a pickup truck carrying two firearms, 350 rounds of ammunition, a machete, and a billy club. His plan? Kidnap either Bo or Sunny. Even Millie Bush, unfairly labeled "ugly" by the *Washingtonian* magazine, and Socks, whose White House supremacy was threatened by the arrival of a puppy, never had to worry about abduction.

MORE ON THE OBAMAS' SUNNY

Sunny, slightly more temperamental than Bo, once bit a White House guest. She also possessed one truly unfortunate habit—defecating outside the president's office. As the former commander in chief recalled to *People* magazine shortly before leaving office, "She knows she's doing wrong. . . . Sometimes I'll be in my office, and I'm doing work, and I'll see this like scurrying. . . . And I got to get up and run before she does her thing, because if I'm too late then there's a little gift that she leaves." (The First Lady added, in defense of Sunny, that the dog hadn't "done her thing" inside for quite some time.) Unlike some earlier presidential pets, Sunny wasn't exiled from the Executive Mansion for her crimes against housebreaking. She continues to live with the Obamas to this day.

When the Obamas acquired Sunny, they made a donation to the Humane Society in her name.

The Obamas spent two terms in the White House. Bo remained with the family as they resumed their lives post-presidency. He lived to be twelve and passed away in 2021. In a series of tweets commenting on the loss of his friend, the former president reflected: "He tolerated all the fuss that came with being in the White House, had a big bark but no bite, loved to jump in the pool in the summer, was unflappable with children, lived for scraps around the dinner table, and had great hair." What a good boy!

11
RESCUE ERA DOGS

COMMANDER + CHAMP + MAJOR BIDEN
German Shepherds

Any animal belonging to the president of the United States becomes by proxy America's pet, and the attention paid to that animal corresponds to its status. Photographers gather to train their lenses on the furry First Pet, and press secretaries field questions about the animal's habits, its likes and dislikes, and even its schedule. When President Joe Biden brought his German shepherd Major to the Executive Mansion, the media focused on something that set the dog apart from all his First Pet forebears. Major is the first presidential dog adopted from a shelter. His ascendancy represents the culmination of a movement that's been growing in the United States for decades and, animal advocates hope, will point the way forward.

While previous presidential pets—LBJ's Yuki and Clinton's cat Socks—were strays who joined their families when found, only Major came from an animal rescue: the no-kill Delaware Humane Association.

Journalist and animal rights activist Jane Velez-Mitchell agrees that a rescue dog in the White House was a hugely significant milestone in the animal rights movement. "It may seem like a small thing that there's a rescue dog in the White House," Velez-Mitchell said, "but it's a big leap." The presidency, in addition to all its political power, serves as a massive cultural signpost. As such, Velez-Mitchell noted, "This really is a breakthrough, having a rescue dog as a presidential companion."

Velez-Mitchell is correct to note that rescues are gaining in popularity. In December of 2020, *Time* named rescue animals the "Pet of the Year," acknowledging Major's upcoming ascension to the White House as well as a surge in pet adoption spurred by the social distancing of the COVID-19 pandemic.

The rise of animal rescues corresponds to the growth of the internet and, even more so, to the development of platforms like Facebook and Twitter. Social media sites allow rescue groups to share photos and stories about incoming adoptees, reaching a wider audience than would be possible otherwise. They can request donations, livestream special events, and spread the word about recently found strays. In many ways, it's become easier than ever to adopt a pet.

Despite the efforts of rescues, misconceptions still drive the market for dog breeding. Some 34 percent of dogs are acquired from breeders each year, with only a combined 29 percent being strays or shelter animals. The Humane Society of the United States reports that between 6 million and 8 million animals will find themselves in a shelter every year. Of the dogs, one in four are purebred. Shelter dogs are often stigmatized; potential pet owners sometimes worry that the animals are in the shelter because of bad behavior that would make them undesirable. This is not true—the Humane Society reports "moving" and "landlord issues" as the most common reasons an animal is surrendered, not behavioral difficulties.

Velez-Mitchell attributes these misconceptions to breeders, who have a vested interest in undermining the work of rescue groups. She points to the genetic health issues that can be common in purebred dogs. "The irony," she says, "is that the stray dogs from the streets are actually healthier than those that are bred in puppy mills and sold."

These societal misconceptions have dire consequences. About half of all animals who enter a shelter are not adopted. Some of those animals—about 710,000—are successfully returned to their homes, but in many municipalities, where animal control is run primarily by law enforcement, stray animals have almost no hope. Many shelters have little budget for or interest in long-term animal care. "You can't even call them high-kill shelters," said Karen Johnson, who worked in the George W. Bush administration before turning her attention to animal welfare issues. "They're like immediate-kill shelters." A dog entering such a facility has one day, maybe two, to be claimed before being euthanized. Though shelter euthanasia is down 25 percent from 2011, it remains a staggeringly high 1.5 million deaths a year.

For this reason, Johnson uses her blog PawsGo and its offshoot *Pawdcast* to celebrate and promote smaller rural shelters. "I know how tight their budgets are," Johnson said. "I know how hard they work." Any extra attention, especially if it results in increased fundraising, is critical to small rescues.

During the initial stages of the COVID-19 pandemic, when most Americans found themselves facing orders to stay at home, many shelters around the country saw an increase in animal adoptions. Madeline Bernstein, president of the Society for the Prevention of Cruelty to Animals Los Angeles, told *Time* magazine: "The animal shelters have been emptied of adoptable animals through either adoptions or fosters, because of what a good time it is, when families are home together during lockdown, to work with a new pet. And it's also a hedge against loneliness."

More than that, as the Humane Society of the United States points out, adopting a pet is often significantly cheaper than buying one. Breeders often charge exorbitant fees, and they rarely provide the spaying or neutering, vaccinations, and microchipping common with rescues. If you adopt an older animal, they may already be trained and housebroken, saving adoptive families even more money.

Jeremy Bernard, who served as the social secretary for President Obama, adopted his dogs from Beagle Freedom Project, which rescues its beagles from laboratory experimentation. He believes that many Americans are just now learning the benefits of animal adoption, and that all rescue dog owners can help spread the word about such benefits. "When I walk my beagles, they get a lot of attention," he said. "When I tell people that they're rescues, there's an immediate interest. It provides people with an example of something they might not have thought of."

With a shelter dog in the White House, animal rescue has finally taken hold of the bully pulpit. There is reason for optimism, even as the need for adoptions remains constant. The cliché says that every dog has his day, and rescue dogs are finally at the forefront of conversation.

DONALD TRUMP
In Office: 2017–2021

POLITICAL PARTY: REPUBLICAN

President Donald Trump was a rarity in American politics. A political outsider with no experience in public service, a billionaire who positioned himself as a man of the people, and an image-conscious media presence who disregarded all advice from his PR handlers, Trump defined the word *unprecedented* as it applies to presidential politics. Among his many unique characteristics: he was the first president in over a century with no dog. He addressed the issue in February of 2019. "I wouldn't mind having one, honestly," he told a crowd of supporters in El Paso, Texas, "but I don't have any time." He added that acquiring a dog for political reasons would feel "phony." Regardless of how one feels about President Trump and his policies, at least he understood that people who aren't fully committed to dog ownership should not get a dog.

In November 2019, President Trump did bring a dog to the Executive Mansion. Conan,

Donald Trump was the first president in more than a century to have no pets during his time in the White House.

a Belgian Malinois trained and handled by American military personnel, had previously been injured during a raid that led to the death of Islamic State leader Abu Bakr al-Baghdadi. "Conan is a tough cookie," Trump told reporters, adding that the dog was "beautiful" and referring to the breed as the "ultimate fighter, ultimate everything." The president awarded a plaque and a medal to the canine hero, whom he had also celebrated in a series of tweets. As the press conference ended, a reporter asked First Lady Melania Trump if the family might adopt Conan for their young son, Barron. According to the *Washington Post*, she "appeared to decline."

Marlon Bundo, the rabbit belonging to Vice President Mike Pence's family, is one of the best-named pets in presidential history.

While the president spoke highly of Conan, it was the vice president who gave the military hero a scratch behind the ears. Politically minded animal lovers were not surprised by the VP's show of canine affection.

In the four long years where no pets of any kind stalked the halls of the White House, Americans turned to Vice President Mike Pence for cute animal stories. Pence, the former governor of Indiana, came to Washington with two cats, a snake, an Australian shepherd named Harley gifted to him by his wife, and much to the delight of Instagram users, a rabbit named Marlon Bundo.

Though Marlon formally belonged to the VP's daughter Charlotte, he garnered significant public attention. Several factors likely aided the rabbit's rise to notoriety: President Trump's lack of a pet, the clever name, and traditional rabbit adorability. The rabbit's Instagram account attracted thousands of followers eager to see how the BOTUS (Bunny of the United States) spent his time at the epicenter of American politics. Charlotte and her mother, Karen Pence, wrote a children's book called *Marlon Bundo's A Day in the Life of the Vice President,* which featured Marlon following "Grampa" Pence through a routine vice-presidential workday. Proceeds from the book—written by Charlotte and illustrated by Second Lady Karen—went to Tracy's Kids (an art therapy program for cancer patients) and A21 (an organization combating human trafficking).

Last Week Tonight with John Oliver issued a parody of the Pence book on March 18, 2018, a day before the Pence book became available. In this version, written by *Last Week* staffer Jill Twiss, the vice-presidential pet meets another male rabbit, Wesley, and falls in love. Designed as a commentary on the vice president's opposition to same-sex marriage and support of gay conversion therapy, Twiss's book benefited charity as well. In this case, the beneficiaries were the Trevor Project (which works to prevent LGBTQIA+ suicide) and AIDS United. Charlotte Pence, rather than take offense, bought a copy of Twiss's book and promoted it on the official Bundo Instagram account. Both

books were bestsellers, though the Twiss book sold 600,000 copies compared to 32,000 for the Pence family book. Having the support of a popular television show can certainly boost sales.

Marlon Bundo's notoriety surpassed the other Pence pets', including that of their Australian shepherd, Harley, whom the VP added to the family in June of 2017.

"I asked my wife for a motorcycle [for Father's Day]," Vice President Pence told the National Association of Manufacturers during an address, "and I got a puppy, so I named him Harley." Of course, naming the little Aussie proved less difficult than trying to decipher what title he should hold. As Karin Brulliard mused in the *Washington Post*: "Pence spokesman Marc Lotter deemed Harley the nation's 'Second Dog,' which seems a bit unfair. There is no First Dog, after all. And if the rabbit is BOTUS, shouldn't Harley be DOTUS?"

Karen Pence took this photo of Vice President Mike Pence after surprising him with Harley the puppy on Father's Day. That same day, the family also adopted a new kitten, named Hazel.

It was obvious that the Pence family adored animals, even if Americans lacked an agreed-upon vocabulary to discuss them. While Instagram went wild for the pets, not everyone shared that enthusiasm. In its January/February 2018 issue, *The Atlantic* quoted an anonymous Trump advisor who claimed to have heard the president disparage Pence's menagerie: "He was embarrassed by it; he thought it was so low-class [that the family brought pets to the VP residence]. He thinks the Pences are yokels." A spokesman for Pence vehemently denied that the president had ever said this.

The Second Rabbit achieved more publicity than any previous vice-presidential pet, but the 2020 election brought another (though less widely known) onetime resident of the Naval Observatory into the spotlight.

JOE BIDEN
In Office: 2021–Present

POLITICAL PARTY: DEMOCRATIC

Champ Biden, a German shepherd, joined the Biden family shortly after long-time Delaware senator Joe Biden became Barack Obama's vice president in 2009. Champ, now accompanied by another shepherd named Major, hoped to transition from the vice-presidential residence to the Executive Mansion.

President Joe Biden really loves German shepherds. Three lived in the White House during his first year in office.

With the canine-loving former vice president slated to run against pet-less President Trump, the subject of presidential dogs inevitably came to the forefront. While the candidates themselves debated the government's response to the COVID-19 pandemic, immigration issues, and environmental policies, a group known as Dog Lovers for Joe released a brief ad showing photos of recent presidents with their dogs, contrasting them with Trump. The ad ends with a photo of the Biden dogs. The implication of the ad was clear: the Trump presidency is an aberration, even on

Major Biden runs around the South Lawn of the White House on January 24, 2021.

the most minute level. Normalcy, according to the ad, includes a canine in the White House, and said normalcy must be restored.

The return of animals to 1600 Pennsylvania Avenue drew a significant amount of attention, and Major's story threw a bright spotlight on the Delaware Humane Association. On January 17, 2021, three days before the inauguration of President Biden, Pumpkin Pet Insurance worked with the animal

Major Biden on the day he was adopted.

rescue to hold a virtual "indoguration" for Major. This event—the first of its kind—set a goal of raising $10,000 for the rescue. Singer Josh Groban performed an original song, and *Today* correspondent Jill Martin served as emcee. With more than 10,000 people watching live, and nearly 100,000 eventually checking out the ceremony on YouTube, the celebration resulted in more than $202,000 raised for the Delaware Humane Association.

The incoming president sought to maximize the apolitical appeal of his dogs as part of his administration's efforts to slow the spread of COVID-19. On Sunday, February 7, 2021, First Lady Jill Biden and her two German shepherds, Champ and Major, appeared in a thirty-second public service announcement during Animal Planet's annual Puppy Bowl, a genial bit of counterprogramming that airs during the Super Bowl. She asked every American to wear a mask when out in public. "We owe it to them to stay healthy," she said, indicating the dogs. It was the highest-profile appearance yet for the First Dogs, who had been in the White House for less than a month. Champ and Major appeared to be the first of a new type of First Pet, born in an era of social media and viral sensations—presidential pets as influencers.

Media attention—as many a disgraced influencer could have told the Biden team—can be a double-edged sword. Within weeks of winning his election, while still preparing for his inauguration, president-elect Biden fractured his foot while playing with Major. The injury—caused by a slip—required Biden to see an orthopedist but was not particularly serious. Because the accident led to only a mild injury, it did not raise concerns about the dog's behavior.

Unfortunately, Major struggled in the transition to life in the White House. On two separate occasions in the early months of the Biden presidency, he nipped staffers, one a Secret Service agent and the other an employee of the National Park Service. These incidents, neither of which broke skin or caused serious harm, are more reminiscent of Barney Bush's nipping of a reporter than they are of Teddy Roosevelt's bull terrier's treeing the French ambassador. Still, the unwanted behavior required correction, and Major moved offsite for additional training.

Saturday Night Live spoofed these biting incidents on March 27, 2021, depicting the German shepherd attacking Second Gentleman Doug Emhoff (played by Martin Short) during a Passover dinner. "Something spooked that hellhound," Short's Emhoff muses upon recovering from the assault.

A series of emails obtained in August 2021 by conservative watchdog (no pun intended) Judicial Watch indicate that Major had been involved in more incidents than previously disclosed to the public. The communications, sent between Secret Service members, describe a daily pattern of nipping that lasted over a week in early March, rather than just the two previously reported occurrences. Fortunately, all injuries were minor. The White House reiterated that Major, as previously reported, has since undergone more extensive training and is continuing to adjust to the White House. None of the newly disclosed bites have happened since this training began.

The president defended Major in an interview with ABC News, saying he was a "sweet dog" acting out of a desire to protect his human from unknown individuals—which, for a dog in a new home filled with staffers, security, and aides, can appear just about anywhere.

In May 2021, *New York* magazine's *Intelligencer* reported that President Biden occasionally sneaked out of the office for some playtime on the South Lawn with his dogs. Like many presidents before him, Biden found some relief from the pressures of the presidency the same way any other pet owner would—by playing with his furry friends. Major, the first shelter dog to live in the White House, feels like a canine version of the American dream. Anyone, the old cliché says, can grow up to be president. Now any dog, no matter their lineage or beginnings, can belong to a president too.

While there is reason for optimism about the growth of rescues nationwide, Major's story did not end in a Fala-like reign as America's dog. In December of 2021, the Biden family announced that, on advice from experts, Major would be rehomed with family friends. In an email to the author sent on December 21, 2021, Michael LaRosa, press secretary to the First Lady, stated that these experts believe "it would be safest for Major to live in a quieter environment," though he also emphasized that the decision was not made in response to any new biting or aggression incidents. The move from Delaware to D.C., combined with the June 2021 death of Biden's other dog, Champ, appears to have been too much for Major to bear.

At first glance, Major's relocation might feel like a rebuke to the rescue movement, as if shelter dogs are uniquely incapable of life in the spotlight. Journalist and animal rights advocate Jane Velez-Mitchell disagrees: "This has nothing to do with his being a rescue dog. The White House is a famously stressful place to live for humans and animals." Indeed, as we have seen in previous chapters, purebred non-shelter dogs like Herbert Hoover's King Tut and FDR's German shepherd, coincidentally named Major as well, have found the Executive Mansion an overwhelming and unhappy home.

The announcement of Major's departure arrived concurrently with images of a new presidential dog named Commander, another German shepherd. This puppy, born on September 1, 2021, was a birthday gift to the president from his brother James and James's wife, Sara. It does not appear that this puppy came from a shelter. While the puppy's provenance might prove disappointing, Commander will hopefully adapt well

Commander arrived at 1600 Pennsylvania Avenue in late December 2021. He is the third German shepherd to live in the Biden White House.

to his new home and his new family. President Biden, battling a pandemic and working to move legislation through a not-always-receptive Congress, can certainly use the new friend.

Within days of his arrival at 1600 Pennsylvania Avenue, Commander had already taken on some of a presidential dog's duties. During a Christmas Eve visit to Children's National Medical Center, President Biden used his cell phone to show inquisitive kids photos of his new dog. On December 25, the puppy joined the president and First Lady for a virtual event thanking members of all branches of the United States military stationed around the globe for their service.

We cannot yet know how much these developments have permanently shifted American attitudes toward pet ownership. Will Major inspire other animal lovers to choose adoption? What are the long-term effects of a generation of pandemic pets? Americans are a pet-loving people, and there are more ways than ever for them to meet their next best friends. Millions of animals are out there in rescue groups, waiting for a chance to fill that role.

OTHER BIDEN PETS

CHAMP: Shortly after being elected to the vice presidency in 2008, Joe Biden and his wife Jill acquired a German shepherd puppy whom they named Champ. The dog lived with them at the Naval Observatory for the entirety of the Obama administration. He loved chasing golf balls and playing with the vice president's grandchildren. Like Millie Bush before him, Champ transitioned to the White House when his human got promoted. Also like Millie, Champ found himself the victim of media trolling. In his case, Newsmax host Greg Kelly used his show to say Champ looked "rough" and in need of a bath. (Kelly's comments were rightfully met with widespread derision.) Through everything, he proved a faithful and loving companion. When he passed away at the Bidens' Delaware home in June of 2021, the family released a statement in praise of Champ: "In our most joyful moments and in our most grief-stricken days, he was there with us, sensitive to our every unspoken feeling and emotion. We love our sweet, good boy, and will miss him always."

WILLOW: In November of 2020, shortly after President Biden's election, *CBS Sunday Morning* host Jane Pauley announced that the Bidens would soon add a cat to the family. In March of 2021, the First Lady, Dr. Jill Biden, told *Today* that a cat was "waiting in the wings." No feline family member has been introduced to the public. In an interview with the *New York Times* published September 19, 2021, the First Lady acknowledged that Major's aggressive behavior and the subsequent training sessions had delayed the cat's arrival. In January 2022, Willow, a tabby, was introduced to the public. She had interacted with the soon-to-be First Lady during a Pennsylvania campaign stop during the 2020 election and was given to the Bidens.

RESOURCES

Beagle Freedom Project (www.bfp.org)

Dedicated to rescuing, rehabilitating, and rehousing dogs used in testing and experimentation, this group also advocates for an end to such animal experimentation.

Delaware Humane Association (www.delawarehumane.org)

This group helped pair Major with then–Vice President Joe Biden, eventually sending the first rescue dog to the White House.

3 Girls Animal Rescue (www.3girlsanimalrescue.com)

Based in Oklahoma, this rescue has saved thousands of dogs and cats from local kill shelters.

GUIDE DOG SCHOOLS

The Seeing Eye (www.seeingeye.org)

The first American school to train dogs and their blind partners how to move freely together through the world at large is located in Morristown, New Jersey.

Guide Dogs of America (www.guidedogsofamerica.org)

Based in Sylmar, California, this organization provides guides to blind individuals at no cost. Recently, they have begun training dogs for veterans battling PTSD as well.

ANIMAL RIGHTS ORGANIZATIONS

The American Society for the Prevention of Cruelty to Animals (www.aspca.org)

North America's oldest Humane Society, the ASPCA helps relocate and shelter animals, works to abolish puppy mills, and promotes legislation to improve animal welfare.

Friends of Animals (www.friendsofanimals.org)

FoA works for animals on several fronts. They have provided over 2.8 million low-cost spay and neuter procedures. They fight to protect wildlife from human threats. They also work to reduce and eradicate animal testing.

The No Kill Advocacy Center (www.nokilladvocacycenter.org)

This group works to promote the no kill shelter model and has thus saved untold thousands of animal lives.

FURTHER INFORMATION

Animal Charity Evaluators (www.animalcharityevaluators.org)

Before you give, you can go to this website to find effective charities related to all aspects of animal welfare.

Jane Unchained (www.janeunchained.com)

Jane Velez-Mitchell founded this animal rights news source, which also advocates a plant-based lifestyle.

PawsGo (www.pawsgo.com)

An online community for women and their dogs, PawsGo promotes an active lifestyle and raises money for animal rescues around the United States.

ACKNOWLEDGMENTS

All-American Dogs exists because a large number of people helped me put it together. This is my first nonfiction book, and I am grateful for the assistance I've received along the way.

First and foremost, I would like to thank my editors, Lisa Sharkey and Maddie Pillari, for their insight, encouragement, and vision. A good editor dramatically improves a manuscript, and I was fortunate enough to have two excellent ones. I'd also like to thank the larger HarperCollins team, including Stephanie Vallejo, Melanie Bedor, Renata De Oliveira, Emilia Marroquin, and Isabella Armus.

Bob Kirsch worked tirelessly to insert my citations into the manuscript, and he shared the wisdom of his experience in the process. Diane Kraut and Alli Goldberg helped me find the photos in this book and secure the appropriate permissions. Without them, this book would be a lot less fun.

Several people generously gave their time for interviews. My eternal thanks to Ari Fleischer, Dana Lewis, Jane Velez-Mitchell, Margaret "Peggy" Foster, Paul Landis, Jimmy Orr, David Almacy, Karen Johnson, Jean Card, Bill Yosses, Dorothy V. Thompson, Stephanie Celiberti, Jeremy Bernard, and Shannon Keith.

My agent, Larry Weissman, provided advice that this novice author needed, and he helped me get past my case of Imposter Syndrome. (Special thanks to Scott Shane for introducing us.)

This opportunity would not have been possible without my friends and Presidential Pet Museum colleagues Bill Helman and Tricia Theis Rogalski. Thanks for bringing me into the world of presidential dogs all those years ago.

My two dogs have greatly reduced my stress during the writing process. Emmy is a wonderful cuddler, and she knows just how to curl up by my feet. Sammy, having been so well trained by Guide Dogs of America, provides steadfast, quiet company everywhere I go. (My cats were equally soothing, though, true to their species, more aloof.)

Finally, heartfelt love and gratitude to my children, Mia and Ian, and my amazing, patient wife, Kristy. The three of you are everything to me.

CREDITS

CHAPTER 1: FOUNDING DOGS

Portrait of George Washington, 1794, by Adolf Ulrik Wertmüller.

National Gallery of Victoria, Melbourne, Felton Bequest, 1922. This digital record has been made available on NGV Collection Online through the generous support of Digitisation Champion Ms. Carol Grigor through Metal Manufactures Limited.

Genl. Lafayette's departure from Mount Vernon. Virginia Estate Mount Vernon, None. [N.Y.: published by E. Farrell, between 1840 and 1860] [Photograph] Retrieved from the Library of Congress, https://www.loc.gov/item/98501910/.

Gift of Mr. and Mrs. Stanley DeForest Scott, 1985. Courtesy of Mount Vernon.

John Adams, [No Date Recorded on Shelflist Card] [Photograph] Retrieved from the Library of Congress, https://www.loc.gov/item/2003679977/.

Stuart, G. A. Adams / from an original painting by Gilbert Stuart. None. [New York: Johnson, Wilson & Co. Publishers, between 1830 and 1860?] [Photograph] Retrieved from the Library of Congress, https://www.loc.gov/item/96525381/.

(ca. 1914) James Monroe, ca. 1914. [Photograph] Retrieved from the Library of Congress, https://www.loc.gov/item/91482930/.

CHAPTER 2: HOUSE-DIVIDED DOGS

(1876) Old Abe, the live war eagle of Wisconsin, from the Centennial. United States, 1876. [Photograph] Retrieved from the Library of Congress, https://www.loc.gov/item/2012650046/.

(ca. 1860) President John Tyler, half-length portrait, facing right, ca. 1860. [Between ca. 1860 and 1865, Printed Later] [Photograph] Retrieved from the Library of Congress, https://www.loc.gov/item/96522383/.

The White House Historical Association (White House Collection).

Image Credit: Courtesy of Lancaster History, Lancaster, Pennsylvania.

Frank Leslie's Illustrated Newspaper, March 1857.
Keith Lance/Getty Images.
Fido by F. W. Ingmire, Springfield, Illinois, ca. 1860.

CHAPTER 3: RECONSTRUCTION AND GILDED AGE DOGS

Public domain.
Brady-Handy Photograph Collection, Library of Congress.
[General Grant & his family]/designed by Fred B. Schell; engraved by Samuel Sartain.
   [Philadelphia]: Daughaday & Becker, ca. 1868.
Courtesy of Rutherford B. Hayes Presidential Library & Museums.
Portrait of Rutherford B. Hayes, ca. 1870–1880.
Brady-Handy photograph collection, Library of Congress, Prints and Photographs
   Division.
National Portrait Gallery, Smithsonian Institution; gift of the Reverend Thomas G.
   Cleveland.
Photo of Benjamin Harrison © 1896 by Pach Brothers and restored by Adam Cuerden.
Johnston, F. B., photographer. White House—Major Russell Harrison and Harrison
   children—Baby McKee and sister on goat cart. Washington, D.C. None. [Between 1889
   and 1893] [Photograph] Retrieved from the Library of Congress, https://www.loc.gov
   /item/97510241/.

CHAPTER 4: PROGRESSIVE ERA DOGS

Jack London, *The Call of the Wild.* New York: Macmillan Company, 1903.
Appleton's Magazine, Vol. 1 (January–June 1903).
Theodore Roosevelt's pet one-legged rooster. None. [Between 1910 and 1920?]
   [Photograph] Retrieved from the Library of Congress, https://www.loc.gov
   /item/2010645533/.
Fawcett, W. (ca. 1903) President Roosevelt's dogs no. 2., ca. 1903. June 25. [Photograph]
   Retrieved from the Library of Congress, https://www.loc.gov/item/2010645538/.
Joaquín Sorolla, public domain, via Wikimedia Commons.
Portrait of Woodrow Wilson, 1919, by Harris & Ewing.

CHAPTER 5: DOGS OF THE ROARING TWENTIES

Terrier Hero of Georgetown, public domain, via Wikimedia Commons.

Warner Brothers, public domain, via Wikimedia Commons.

National Photo Company, public domain, via Wikimedia Commons.

Portrait of Calvin Coolidge by George Grantham Bell.

Seward, Geo. M., and Edna Bell Seward. "Laddie Boy He's Gone." 1923: n. pag. Print.

Courtesy of Universal History Archive/contributor.

National Photo Company, public domain, via Wikimedia Commons.

Herbert E. French, public domain, via Wikimedia Commons.

CHAPTER 6: NEW DEAL DOGS

Mrs. Dorothy Harrison Eustis, half-length portrait, standing, on ship?, facing slightly right. None. [Between 1904 and 1924] [Photograph] Retrieved from the Library of Congress, https://www.loc.gov/item/94508341/.

© 2021 The Seeing Eye®.

Portrait of Franklin Delano Roosevelt, 1932, by Vincenzo Laviosa.

Bettmann/Getty Images.

Presidential Portrait of Harry S. Truman, 1945, by Greta Kempton.

Harry S. Truman Library & Museum.

CHAPTER 7: COLD WAR DOGS

Robert Knudsen. White House Photographs. Courtesy of John F. Kennedy Presidential Library and Museum, Boston.

Robert Knudsen. White House Photographs. Courtesy of John F. Kennedy Presidential Library and Museum, Boston.

Official White House portrait of U.S. President Dwight D. Eisenhower, 1959.

Dwight D. Eisenhower Presidential Library and Museum/NARA, National Park Service.

Photograph of John F. Kennedy in the Oval Office, 1963, by Cecil Stoughton.

Robert Knudsen. White House Photographs. Courtesy of John F. Kennedy Presidential Library and Museum, Boston.

Teknoraver, CC BY-SA 4.0 <https://creativecommons.org/licenses/by-sa/4.0>, via Wikimedia Commons.

Photographer unknown. Jacqueline Bouvier Kennedy Onassis Personal Papers. Courtesy of John F. Kennedy Presidential Library and Museum, Boston.

Abbie Rowe. White House Photographs. Courtesy of John F. Kennedy Presidential Library and Museum, Boston.

Robert Knudsen. White House Photographs. Courtesy of John F. Kennedy Presidential Library and Museum, Boston.

Robert L. Knudsen [Cecil Stoughton]. Jacqueline Bouvier Kennedy Onassis Personal Papers. Courtesy of John F. Kennedy Presidential Library and Museum, Boston.

Cecil Stoughton. White House Photographs. Courtesy of John F. Kennedy Presidential Library and Museum, Boston.

LBJ Library; photo by Cecil Stoughton.

LBJ Library; photo by Yoichi Okamoto.

Photo portrait of President Lyndon B. Johnson in the Oval Office, leaning on a chair, 1964, by Arnold Newman.

LBJ Library.

CHAPTER 8: DOGS OF THE SEVENTIES

Presidential Portrait of President Richard Nixon between 1969 and 1974 by Department of Defense.

Everett Collection/Alamy Stock Photos.

W. K. Leffler, photographer. Courtesy of Library of Congress, https://www.loc.gov /item/2019631773/.

Nixon White House Photographs, 1/20/1969–8/9/1974. Collection: White House Photo Office Collection (Nixon Administration), 1/20/1969–8/9/1974.

Photo by Robert L. Knudsen. Courtesy of National Archives and Records Administration via Wikimedia Commons.

Presidential Portrait of Gerald Ford, 1974, by David Hume Kennerly.

White House Photograph. Courtesy of Gerald R. Ford Library.

Courtesy of Gerald R. Ford Library.

A Polaroid Polacolor portrait of Jimmy Carter, 1979, by Ansel Adams.

Courtesy of Jimmy Carter Library.

White House photographer, public domain, via Wikimedia Commons.

CHAPTER 9: END-OF-THE-CENTURY DOGS

Official White House portrait of President Reagan, 1981.

Courtesy of Ronald Reagan Library.

Series: Reagan White House Photographs, 1/20/1981–1/20/1989. Collection: White House Photographic Collection, 1/20/1981–1/20/1989.

Courtesy of Ronald Reagan Library.

White House (Michael Sargent), public domain, via Wikimedia Commons.

Portrait of President George H. W. Bush between 1958 and 1981.

Courtesy of George Bush Presidential Library and Museum/NARA.

George Bush Presidential Library and Museum.

Portrait of President Bill Clinton, 1993, by USAID, Historical Archive.

White House Photo/Barbara Kinney.

CHAPTER 10: NEW MILLENNIUM DOGS

Tomasz Sienicki [user: tsca, mail: tomasz.sienicki at gmail.com], CC BY-SA 3.0 <http://creativecommons.org/licenses/by-sa/3.0/>, via Wikimedia Commons.

Portrait of George W. Bush by Eric Draper.

White House Photo [Kimberlee Hewitt].

White House Photo [Shealah Craighead].

White House Photo [Joyce Boghosian].

Official White House portrait of Barack Obama, 2012, by Pete Souza.

American Photo Archive/Alamy Stock Photo.

White House Photo [Chuck Kennedy].

White House Photo [Chuck Kennedy].

Courtesy of Barack Obama Presidential Library.

The White House from Washington, D.C., public domain, via Wikimedia Commons.

CHAPTER 11: RESCUE ERA DOGS

Official White House portrait of President Donald J. Trump, 2017, by Shealah Craighead.

© 2018 Stephanie Gomez Carter/Delaware Human Association.

White House Photo by Hannah MacInnis.

Portrait of Joe Biden, 2013, by David Lienemann.

© Karen Pence.

White House Photo/Alamy Stock Photo.

Photo portrait of Bill Clinton with Buddy on the South Lawn, 1999, by Barbara Kinney.

Photo of Commander Biden, 2021, by White House.

NOTES

CHAPTER 1: FOUNDING DOGS

7 from 206 BCE to 220 CE: Kallie Szczepanski, "History of the Pekingese Dog," ThoughtCo, January 29, 2020, accessed September 22, 2021, https://www.thoughtco.com/history-of-the-pekingese-dog-195234.

7 "damn your dogs": James Breig, "The Eighteenth Century Goes to the Dogs," *CW Journal,* Autumn 2004, accessed March 26, 2021, https://research.colonialwilliamsburg.org/foundation/journal/Autumn04/dogs.cfm.

7 to accept the throne: "Royal Family Members Who Love Pugs," Lucky Pug, April 27, 2019, accessed September 12, 2021, https://www.luckypug.com/famous-pugs/notable-royal-family-members-who-love-pugs/.

7 with the British monarchy: Ed Pearce, "Pug," Encyclopedia of Trivia, May 21, 2017, accessed March 28, 2021, https://encyclopaediaoftrivia.blogspot.com/2017/05/pug.html.

7 the arrival of Europeans: Barbara van Asch et al., "Pre-Columbian Origins of Native American Dog Breeds, with Only Limited Replacement by European Dogs, Confirmed by mtDNA Analysis," *Proceedings of the Royal Society B* 280, no. 1766 (2013): 20131142, accessed March 30, 2021, https://royalsocietypublishing.org/doi/10.1098/rspb.2013.1142.

9 those dogs who had died: Breig, "The Eighteenth Century."

9 "and ready money": Breig, "The Eighteenth Century."

9 one's elevated station: Breig, "The Eighteenth Century."

9 in Great Britain during this time: Breig, "The Eighteenth Century."

9 no natural predators in North America: Alex Robinson, "The Hog Dogs of Alabama," *Outdoor Life,* August 10, 2018, accessed March 29, 2021, https://www.outdoorlife.com/hog-hunting-dogs/.

10 protecting the equipment from thieves: Anna Burke, "What Was the Dalmatian Bred to Do?" American Kennel Club, March 8, 2017, accessed March 30, 2021, https://www.akc.org/expert-advice/lifestyle/dalmation-breed-facts/.

12 considered to be excellent: Breig, "The Eighteenth Century."

14 bred the dog himself: Stanley Coren, "George Washington: President, General and Dog Breeder," *Psychology Today,* January 2, 2009, accessed September 13, 2021, https://www.psychologytoday.com/us/blog/canine-corner/200901/george-washington-president-general-and-dog-breeder.

14 second term as president: Coren, "George Washington: President, General."

15 a representative on the general's farms: "Soldier, Statesman, Dog Lover: George Washington's Pups," Mount Vernon, accessed March 30, 2021, https://www.mountvernon.org/george-washington/facts/washington-stories/soldier-statesman-dog-lover-george-washingtons-pups/.

15 the aforementioned Sweet Lips were hounds: "Soldier, Statesman."

15 when he was home: "Soldier, Statesman."

17 to their new owner: Mary Brigid of Barrett, "Presidential Menageries: George Washington, Hound Dogs, and Super Mules," Our White House, 2016, accessed March 28, 2021, https://ourwhitehouse.org/presidential-menageries/.

17 did not attack one another: Barrett, "Presidential Menageries."

17 less than amused: Barrett, "Presidential Mcnagcries."

17 outside in the spring and summer: Mary V. Thompson, email message to the author, January 28, 2021.

18 "and the dogs hanged": "From George Washington to Anthony Whitting, December 16, 1792," National Archives, Founders Online, accessed August 31, 2021, https://founders.archives.gov/documents/Washington/05-11-02-0315.

18 easy to take in: Thompson email.

19 breeders even today: John Ensminger, "The Dogs of George Washington and the Less Fortunate Ones of His Slaves," Academia.edu, accessed September 12, 2021, https://www.academia.edu/19520501/The_Dogs_of_George_Washington_and_the_Less_Fortunate_Ones_of_His_Slaves.

21 "you must love my dog": "From Abigail Smith Adams to Caroline Amelia Smith De Windt, February 26, 1811," National Archives, Founders Online, accessed March 30, 2021, https://founders.archives.gov/documents/Adams/99-03-02-1918.

22 "whenever one appears": "From Abigail Smith Adams."

23 could sing some arias: Sarah Gerrity, "The Crazy, Heartwarming, Surprising Pets Who've Lived in the White House Since the Start," Daily Paws, January 19, 2021, accessed August 28, 2021, https://www.dailypaws.com/dogs-puppies/dog-photos/presidential-pets.

23 now-familiar name, the White House: Gerrity, "The Crazy, Heartwarming, Surprising Pets."

25 a letter to his daughter: "James Monroe's Spaniel," Presidential Pet Museum, accessed March 22, 2021, https://www.presidentialpetmuseum.com/james-monroes-spaniel/.

25 "more than the Spaniel": "James Monroe's Spaniel," Presidential Pet Museum.

CHAPTER 2: HOUSE-DIVIDED DOGS

27 a show of animal wisdom: Kate Kelly, "Dog Jack, Mascot and Volunteer for the Union," America Comes Alive, accessed August 24, 2021, https://americacomesalive.com/dog-jack-mascot-volunteer-union/.

27 for his comrades: Kelly, "Dog Jack."

28 during the chaos of fighting: "Animal Mascots of the Civil War," City of Alexandria, Virginia, February 4, 2021, accessed August 23, 2021, https://www.alexandriava.gov/historic/fortward/default.aspx?id=40198.

28 the Wisconsin State Capitol: "Animal Mascots of the Civil War."

29 silkworms at the White House: "Louisa Adams Biography," National First Ladies' Library, accessed August 24, 2021, http://www.firstladies.org/biographies/firstladies.aspx?biography=6.

29 throughout the northeastern United States: Paul Heller, "The Great Silkworm Excitement in the Green Mountains," *Barre Montpelier* [VT] *Times Argus*, September 2, 2019, accessed August 24, 2021, https://www.timesargus.com/news/local/the-great-silkworm-excitement-in-the-green-mountains/article_9afe95cf-0f56-5a23-9f5b-ca09955bc382.html.

29 and is likely apocryphal: Howard Dorre, "John Quincy Adams's Pet Alligator Was a Crock," Plodding Through the Presidents, February 19, 2018, accessed August 23, 2021, https://www.ploddingthroughthepresidents.com/2018/02/john-quincy-adams-pet-alligator-is-crock.html.

29 disrupted the proceedings: Holly Meyer, "Andrew Jackson's Funeral Drew Thousands, 1 Swearing Parrot," Nashville *Tennessean,* June 8, 2015, accessed August 24, 2021, https://www.tennessean.com/story/news/2015/06/07/andrew-jacksons-funeral-drew-thousands-swearing-parrot/28664493/.

30 valuable gifts from foreign leaders: Erick Trickey, "Move Over, Trump: This President's Two Lions Set Off the Greatest Emoluments Debate," *Washington Post,* September 28, 2018, https://www.washingtonpost.com/news/retropolis/wp/2018/07/22/move-over-trump-this-presidents-two-lions-were-the-center-of-the-greatest-emoluments-debate/.

32 pair of Irish wolfhounds: AZ Animals Staff, "Presidential Dogs: The Complete Guide to the First Dogs of the U.S.," AZ Animals, December 11, 2020, accessed August 24, 2021, https://a-z-animals.com/blog/first-dogs-presidents-dogs/.

32 the American consul in Naples: Roy Rowan and Brooke Janis, *First Dogs: American Presidents and Their Best Friends* (New York: Algonquin Books, 2009), 34.

32 "such a pet for a gift": Rowan and Janis, *First Dogs,* 34.

33 required "attention and discipline": Rowan and Janis, *First Dogs,* 34.

35 "puppy of the smallest kind": "Franklin Pierce's Seven Small Dogs," Presidential Pet Museum, August 2021, https://www.presidentialpetmuseum.com/franklin-pierces-seven-small-dogs/.

36 around in his pocket: "Franklin Pierce's Seven Small Dogs."

36 gave the others to friends: "Franklin Pierce's Seven Small Dogs."

37 near the very bottom of the list: U.S. News Staff, "Ranking America's Worst Presidents," *U.S. News & World Report,* November 6, 2019, accessed August 24, 2021, https://www.usnews.com/news/special-reports/the-worst-presidents/articles/ranking-americas-worst-presidents.

38 a downturned punch bowl: Townrow, "The President's Puppy."

38 as much as possible: Townrow, "The President's Puppy."

38 Pennsylvania Avenue home: Stephanie Townrow, "The President's Puppy," LancasterHistory, March 23, 2020, accessed August 24, 2021, https://www.lancasterhistory.org/the-presidents-puppy/.

38 upon his return: Townrow, "The President's Puppy."

39 "attachment to his master": Townrow, "The President's Puppy."

39 with one eye open: Townrow, "The President's Puppy."

39 of a bear: AZ Animals Staff, "Presidential Dogs: The Complete Guide."

40 any part of the animal: Arin Greenwood, "Abraham Lincoln Obsessed Over His Dog Just Like You Do," HuffPost, April 14, 2015, accessed August 25, 2021, https://www.huffpost.com/entry/abraham-lincoln-dog-animal-lover_n_7055640.

40 filled him with regret: Greenwood, "Abraham Lincoln Obsessed."

40 a yellow mutt: Kate Kelly, "Abraham Lincoln's Dog, Fido," America Comes Alive!, August 24, 2021, https://americacomesalive.com/abraham-lincolns-dog-fido/.

40 to the local barbershop: Kelly, "Abraham Lincoln's Dog."

41 Willie and Tad: Kelly, "Abraham Lincoln's Dog."

42 played with Willie and Tad: "Sangamon County History: Was Stabbing Abraham Lincoln's Dog Intentional? Accounts Differ," Springfield [IL] *State Journal-Register,* September 12, 2015, accessed August 25, 2021, https://www.sj-r.com/article/20150912/NEWS/150919825.

42 along with the dog: Kelly, "Abraham Lincoln's Dog."

44 the fallen president: Kelly, "Abraham Lincoln's Dog."

44 tourists to take home: Kelly, "Abraham Lincoln's Dog."

44 from the table as well: Matthew Dessem, "All the Presidents' Pets," *Slate,* January 31, 2021, accessed March 22, 2021, https://slate.com/culture/2021/01/presidential-pets-best-ever-ranked.amp.

45 found days later, dead: "Sangamon County History."

45 not a vegetarian: Greenwood, "Abraham Lincoln Obsessed."

CHAPTER 3: RECONSTRUCTION AND GILDED AGE DOGS

47 discarded by arriving sailors: Abigail Slater, "How an Ancient Military Staple Became Alaska's Favorite Cracker," Turnagain Currents, March 19, 2021, https://turnagain.alaskapacific.edu/how-an-ancient-military-staple-became-alaskas-favorite-cracker/.

47 mass-produced dog food ever manufactured: Dashka Slater, "Who Made That Dog Biscuit?" *New York Times,* August 1, 2014, https://www.nytimes.com/2014/08/03/magazine/who-made-that-dog-biscuit.html.

47 actual meat source: "The History of Commercial Pet Food: A Great American Marketing Story," The Farmer's Dog, March 1, 2017, accessed April 22, 2021, https://www.thefarmersdog.com/digest/the-history-of-commercial-pet-food-a-great-american-marketing-story/.

47 well-to-do English gentlemen: Slater, "Who Made That Dog Biscuit?"

47 puppies, young dogs, and seniors: "The History of Commercial Pet Food."

48 journal of the American Kennel Club: "The History of Commercial Pet Food."

52 no such difficulties: "Ulysses S. Grant's Rosie," Presidential Pet Museum, accessed April 14, 2021, https://www.presidentialpetmuseum.com/ulysses-s-grants-rosie/.

52 appropriately named Faithful: Amy Squire, "First Pets: Four-legged or Feathered Friends of President Ulysses Grant," *Newsmax,* January 23, 2016, accessed April 5, 2021, https://www.newsmax.com/fastfeatures/president-ulysses-grant-pets/2016/01/23/id/710590/.

52 dog suffered an untimely demise: Brandy Arnold, "First Dogs: The Long Legacy of Dogs in the White House," The Dogington Post, January 20, 2021, accessed April 22, 2021, https://www.dogingtonpost.com/first-dogs-the-long-legacy-of-dogs-in-the-white -house/.

53 as "Lemonade Lucy": Kate Kelly, "The Dogs of Rutherford B. Hayes," America Comes Alive!, accessed August 27, 2021, https://americacomesalive.com/the-dogs-of -rutherford-b-hayes/.

54 "prevention of these abuses": "1878 Rutherford B. Hayes—American Humane Association," State of the Union History, April 27, 2021, http://www .stateoftheunionhistory.com/2015/07/1878-rutherford-b-hayes-amercan-humane.html.

55 any significant period of absence: "Grim," Presidential Pet Museum, November 15, 2013, accessed April 15, 2021, https://www.presidentialpetmuseum.com/pets/grim/.

55 he stood his ground: "Grim," Presidential Pet Museum.

55 would stop for him: Kelly, "The Dogs of Rutherford B. Hayes."

56 the late beloved Grim: Kelly, "The Dogs of Rutherford B. Hayes."

56 or misbehavior exists: Kelly, "The Dogs of Rutherford B. Hayes."

56 mockingbird, and a goat: Kelly, "The Dogs of Rutherford B. Hayes."

56 "our mode of life": "Grim," Presidential Pet Museum.

57 Garfield's election in 1880: Chris Woodyard, "Veto Goes Mad," Haunted Ohio, September 18, 2018, accessed March 17, 2021, http://hauntedohiobooks.com/news /animal-tales/veto-goes-mad-14953/.

57 antipathy to the legislation: Woodyard, "Veto Goes Mad."

58 "began his letter again": Dessem, "All the Presidents' Pets."

58 candidate for the White House: Candice Millard, *Destiny of the Republic: A Tale of Madness, Medicine and the Murder of a President* (New York: Audible, 2011). Audiobook.

59 travel to Washington, D.C.: Woodyard, "Veto Goes Mad."

59 which eventually killed him: Millard, *Destiny of the Republic.*

60 "who took him away at once": Woodyard, "Veto Goes Mad."

60 beast could be calmed: Woodyard, "Veto Goes Mad."

61 if not their barn: Woodyard, "Veto Goes Mad."

62 "were for bigger game": Kate Kelly, "Grover Cleveland's Dogs and Other Pets," America Comes Alive!, accessed April 23, 2021, https://americacomesalive.com/grover-clevelands-dogs-pets/.

63 in November and December: Kelly, "Grover Cleveland's Dogs."

63 hares on the White House grounds: Casey Bickford, "First Pets: Four-Legged or Feathered Friends of President Grover Cleveland," *Newsmax,* November 22, 2015, accessed April 30, 2021, https://www.newsmax.com/fastfeatures/president-grover-cleveland-pets/2015/11/22/id/703208/.

63 game chickens and exotic goldfish: Bickford, "First Pets."

64 a Saint Bernard and a poodle: "Cleveland's Summer House," *New York Times,* July 13, 1891.

64 the family's Massachusetts home: "Grover Cleveland's Saint Bernard," Presidential Pet Museum, August 28, 2021, https://www.presidentialpetmuseum.com/grover-clevelands-saint-bernard/.

64 "hours of the night": Dessem, "All the Presidents' Pets."

65 Mr. Reciprocity and Mr. Protection: "Presidential Pets (1860–1921)," Bush White House Archives, accessed April 27, 2021, https://georgewbush-whitehouse.archives.gov/president/holiday/historicalpets1/02-js.html.

66 a collie mix named Dash: "Presidential Pets," Bush White House Archives.

66 played with Dash too often: Kate Kelly, "The Pets in the Benjamin Harrison White House," America Comes Alive!, accessed April 29, 2021, https://americacomesalive.com/the-pets-in-the-benjamin-harrison-white-house/.

66 rather than more sophisticated fare: Kelly, "The Pets in the Benjamin Harrison White House."

CHAPTER 4: PROGRESSIVE ERA DOGS

69 Anna Sewell's *Black Beauty*: Michele Norris, "How 'Black Beauty' Changed the Way We See Horses," *All Things Considered,* NPR, November 2, 2012, accessed May 11, 2021, https://www.npr.org/2012/11/02/163971063/how-black-beauty-changed-the -way-we-see-horses.

69 could not protect themselves: Norris, "How 'Black Beauty' Changed."

70 "Real and Sham Natural History": Gerald Carson, "T.R. and the Nature Fakers," *American Heritage* 22, no. 2 (1971), accessed May 11, 2021, https://www .americanheritage.com/tr-and-nature-fakers.

71 under the title "Nature Fakers": Carson, "T.R. and the Nature Fakers."

71 portrayals of animal behavior: Carson, "T.R. and the Nature Fakers."

72 "interesting reptiles and fishes": "Theodore Roosevelt," National Park Service, accessed August 29, 2021, https://www.nps.gov/people/life-of-theodore-roosevelt.htm.

73 the horror of the family maid: Darrin Lunde, *The Naturalist: Theodore Roosevelt, A Lifetime of Exploration, and the Triumph of American Natural History* (New York: Random House Audio, 2016). Audiobook.

74 with his son Kermit: Lisa Peterson, "Jack the Manchester Terrier—A Member of Teddy Roosevelt's Family," Lisa Unleashed, November 2, 2015, accessed May 17, 2021, https:// lisaunleashed.com/2015/11/02/jack-the-manchester-terrier-a-member-of-teddy roosevelts-family/.

74 until he ran away: Peterson, "Jack the Manchester Terrier."

76 in the same letter: "Letter from Theodore Roosevelt to Alice Roosevelt, May 6, 1905," Theodore Roosevelt Center, accessed May 22, 2021, https://www.theodoreroosevelt center.org/Research/Digital-Library/Record/ImageViewer?libID=o283320&imae No=1.

76 Sagamore Hill for reburial: Peterson, "Jack the Manchester Terrier."

77 Roosevelt's fondness for terriers: "Standard of the Teddy Roosevelt Terrier," American Kennel Club, July 3, 2019, accessed August 30, 2021, https://s3.amazonaws.com/cdn -origin-etr.akc.org/wp-content/uploads/2017/11/23091816/Official-Standard-of-the -Teddy-Roosevelt-Terrier-07.03.19.pdf.

78 considered "the strongest character": Theodore Roosevelt, *The Autobiography of Theodore Roosevelt,* Digireads.com, 2011, 190.

78 "Roman candles, and firecrackers": Roosevelt, *Autobiography*, 190.

78 by climbing a tree: Mark Derr, *A Dog's History of America: How Our Best Friend Explored, Conquered, and Settled a Continent* (New York: North Point Press, 2004), 244.

79 in the pursuit: Derr, *A Dog's History of America*, 244.

79 later named Manchu: "The Roosevelt Pets," National Park Service, accessed August 30, 2021, https://www.nps.gov/thrb/learn/historyculture/the-roosevelt-pets.htm.

79 "stable room for any more": "Letter from Theodore Roosevelt to Alfred S. Rollo," December 22, 1902, Theodore Roosevelt Center, accessed May 22, 2021, https://www.theodorerooseveltcenter.org/Research/Digital-Library/Record?libID=o183781.

81 after the singer: "William Taft's Caruso," Presidential Pet Museum, accessed May 20, 2021, https://www.presidentialpetmuseum.com/william-tafts-caruso/.

83 Some websites: "Woodrow Wilson's Davie," Presidential Pet Museum, accessed May 21, 2021, https://www.presidentialpetmuseum.com/woodrow-wilsons-davie/.

83 a woman named: Helen Bones, "Dogs," April 26, 2019, Woodrow Wilson Presidential Library, accessed May 20, 2021, https://www.woodrowwilson.org/blog/2019/4/26/dogs.

84 the White House rosebushes: Dessem, "All the Presidents' Pets."

84 Wilson's health problems: William Hazelgrove, *Madam President: The Secret Presidency of Edith Wilson* (New York: Blackstone Audio, 2016). Audiobook.

85 bull terrier named Bruce: Bones, "Dogs," Woodrow Wilson Presidential Library.

85 for the ailing president: "Woodrow Wilson's Bruce," Presidential Pet Museum, accessed August 30, 2021, https://www.presidentialpetmuseum.com/woodrow-wilsons-bruce/.

CHAPTER 5: DOGS OF THE ROARING TWENTIES

87 on movie tickets: "The Rise of Hollywood and the Arrival of Sound," Digital History, 2021, accessed May 30, 2021, https://www.digitalhistory.uh.edu/topic_display.cfm?tcid=124.

87 the population of the United States: "The Rise of Hollywood."

87 named Rin Tin Tin: "The Rise of Hollywood."

87 dogs to the foreground: NPR Staff, "Rin Tin Tin: A Silent Film Star on Four Legs," National Public Radio, *Fresh Air,* January 9, 2012, accessed June 8, 2021, https://www.npr.org/2012/01/09/144319530/rin-tin-tin-a-silent-film-star-on-four-legs.

87 a reward for obedience: Susan Orlean, *Rin Tin Tin: The Life and the Legend* (New York: Simon & Schuster Audio, 2011). Audiobook.

88 appearing in films: Orlean, *Rin Tin Tin.*

89 and military work: Denise Flaim, "German Shepherd Dog History: Origins of the Working Breed," American Kennel Club, September 5, 2021, accessed June 7, 2021, https://www.akc.org/expert-advice/dog-breeds/german-shepherd-dog-history/.

89 battlefields full of corpses: NPR Staff, "Rin Tin Tin."

90 at the box office: Orlean, *Rin Tin Tin.*

91 "brave and devoted dog": Diane Tedeschi, "The White House's First Celebrity Dog," *Smithsonian Magazine,* January 22, 2009, https://www.smithsonianmag.com/history/the-white-houses-first-celebrity-dog-48373830/.

93 Harding's first cabinet meeting: Tedeschi, "The White House's First Celebrity Dog."

93 any cabinet secretary: Doug Capra, "Laddie Boy and President Warren G. Harding's 1923 Visit to Alaska Part 2," *Seward Journal,* October 22, 2020, accessed May 30, 2021, https://www.sewardjournal.com/features/sewards_history/laddie-boy-and-president-warren-g-harding-s-1923-visit-to-alaska-part-2/article_e74cd556-1499-11eb-9da6-8be9cd582b91.html.

93 his master without incident: Kate Kelly, "Laddie Boy, Warren Harding's Dog," America Comes Alive!, accessed June 2, 2021, https://americacomesalive.com/laddie-boy-warren-hardings-dog/.

93 highly prized collector's items: Tedeschi, "The White House's First Celebrity Dog."

94 "no such aspirations": Kelly, "Laddie Boy."

94 the local Toledo press: Kelly, "Laddie Boy."

94 stuffed animals of his dog: Tedeschi, "The White House's First Celebrity Dog."

95 "make Laddie Boy understand": Tedeschi, "The White House's First Celebrity Dog."

95 "glimpse of him again": Tedeschi, "The White House's First Celebrity Dog."

97 on fifteen separate occasions: Kelly, "Laddie Boy."

97 she viewed as a son: Tedeschi, "The White House's First Celebrity Dog."

100 admitted in his autobiography: "Calvin Coolidge's Dog, Prudence Prim," Presidential Pet Museum, January 4, 2014, accessed June 14, 2021, https://www.presidentialpetmuseum.com/pets/coolidge-prudence-prim/.

100 "great courage and fidelity": Dessem, "All the Presidents' Pets."

102 "wouldn't pick up with me": C. Brian Kelly with Ingrid Smyer, *Best Little Stories from the White House: More Than 100 True Stories* (Nashville, TN: Cumberland House, 2012), 157.

102 he quieted down: Margaret Truman, *White House Pets* (New York: David McKay Co., 1969), ebook.

102 for her beloved dog: "Calvin Coolidge's Dog, Prudence Prim."

103 him to trip and fall: Truman, *White House Pets.*

103 "commune with his children": "Calvin Coolidge's Dog, Prudence Prim."

103 "on the hither shore": Dessem, "All the Presidents' Pets."

104 "a surly disposition": Truman, *White House Pets.*

104 company the dog openly enjoyed: Truman, *White House Pets.*

104 snout in everyone's business: Truman, *White House Pets.*

104 the First Lady's bedroom: Truman, *White House Pets.*

104 many dogs roamed free: kcgrier, "Dog Muzzles and City Dogs, 1900," The Pet Historian, August 20, 215, accessed August 29, 2021, https://thepethistorian.com/2015/08/20/dog-muzzles-and-city-dogs-1900/.

104 live out his days: Truman, *White House Pets.*

105 nickname "Terrible Tim": Truman, *White House Pets.*

105 Blackberry's constant baying: Truman, *White House Pets.*

105 to his daughter-in-law: Kate Kelly, "The Coolidge Dogs (and Other Animals)," America Comes Alive!, accessed August 30, 2021, https://americacomesalive.com/the-coolidge-dogs-and-other-animals/.

105 "him and him alone": "Calvin Coolidge's King Cole," Presidential Pet Museum, accessed June 11, 2021, https://www.presidentialpetmuseum.com/calvin-coolidges-king-cole/.

105 teacher from Kentucky: "Coolidge's King Cole."

106 live with her mother: "Calvin Coolidge's Boston Beans," Presidential Pet Museum, accessed June 11, 2021, https://www.presidentialpetmuseum.com/calvin-coolidges-boston-beans/.

106 the trailblazing frontierswoman: Truman, *White House Pets.*

106 christened dog clean: "Calamity Jane," Presidential Pet Museum, March 29, 2014, accessed August 22, 2021, https://www.presidentialpetmuseum.com/pets/calamity-jane/.

106 better fit his needs: "Calvin Coolidge's Palo Alto," Presidential Pet Museum, accessed August 30, 2021, https://www.presidentialpetmuseum.com/calvin-coolidges-palo-alto/.

106 is known about her: Truman, *White House Pets.*

108 business in Belgium: Truman, *White House Pets.*

108 printed and distributed: Truman, *White House Pets.*

108 from scattering them: Truman, *White House Pets.*

109 aggressive toward strangers: Truman, *White House Pets.*

109 Walcott of Connecticut: "Hoover White House Pets," Herbert Hoover Presidential Library, accessed June 16, 2021, https://hoover.archives.gov/hoovers/first-familys-pets.

109 by a sympathetic populace: Truman, *White House Pets.*

109 "all of it was bad": David Greenberg, "Calvin Coolidge: Domestic Affairs," Miller Center, accessed August 28, 2021, https://millercenter.org/president/coolidge/domestic -affairs.

110 "barked too much": "Hoover White House Pets."

110 one of Hoover's secretaries: "Hoover White House Pets."

111 Marine guards at Camp Rapidan: "Hoover White House Pets."

111 better suited the dog: "Hoover White House Pets."

111 time in office: "Hoover White House Pets."

111 granddaughter, Peggy Ann: "Hoover White House Pets."

CHAPTER 6: NEW DEAL DOGS

113 inattentive and unreliable: "Morris Frank and Buddy," Atlas Obscura, accessed June 4, 2021, https://www.atlasobscura.com/places/morris-frank-and-buddy-statue.

113 regaining his independence: "Morris Frank and Buddy."

114 "at a new life": Jill Lenk Schilp, *Dogs in Health Care: Pioneering Animal-Human Partnership* (New York: McFarland, 2019), 78.

115 dogs offered the blind: "Morris Frank and Buddy."

115 out of Nashville: "History," The Seeing Eye, accessed June 17, 2021, https://www .seeingeye.org/about-us/history.html.

115 where it remains: "History."

115 independence to their partners: "Morris Frank and Buddy."

115 Calvin Coolidge and Herbert Hoover: "Blind Pioneer—Morris Frank." The Accidental Talmudist, January 11, 2017, accessed June 3, 2021, https://www.accidentaltalmudist .org/heroes/2017/01/11/the-blind-pioneer-and-his-very-special-dog/.

115 in commercial air travel: "Morris Frank and Buddy."

117 partnerships in the United States today: "The Seeing Eye by the Numbers," The Seeing Eye, accessed June 4, 2021, https://www.seeingeye.org/assets/pdfs/the-seeing-eye-by-the-numbers.pdf.

117 work at The Seeing Eye: "Morris Frank and Buddy."

118 November of that year: "Fala Biography," Franklin Delano Roosevelt Presidential Library and Museum, accessed June 1, 2021, https://www.fdrlibrary.org/fala.

120 the president's ancestors: "Fala Biography."

120 popular breed of the 1930s: AKC Staff, "Top 10 Dog Breeds of the 1930s," American Kennel Club, February 13, 2015, accessed August 30, 2021, https://www.akc.org/expert-advice/lifestyle/top-ten-breeds-of-the-1930s/.

120 his Hyde Park estate: "Fala Biography."

120 prime minister Winston Churchill: "Fala Biography."

121 the foot of Roosevelt's bed: "Fala Biography."

121 "I love my dog": *Fala: The President's Dog*, MGM, 1943.

122 during awards season: *Princess O'Rourke,* Warner Bros., 1943, Internet Movie Database, accessed August 22, 2021, https://www.imdb.com/title/tt0036277/.

122 off the coast of Alaska: Andrew Glass, "FDR Defends Fala Against GOP Attack, September 23, 1944," *Politico,* September 23, 2016, accessed June 1, 2021, https://www.politico.com/story/2016/09/fdr-defends-fala-against-gop-attack-sept-23-1944-228362.

123 a shipload of seamen: Glass, "FDR Defends Fala."

123 auteur Orson Welles: Glass, "FDR Defends Fala."

123 "statements about my dog": Glass, "FDR Defends Fala."

124 First Lady Eleanor: "FDR's Other Scottish Terrier, Meggie," Presidential Pet Museum, February 29, 2016, accessed June 3, 2021, https://www.presidentialpetmuseum.com/pets/fdr-dog-meggie/.

124 news syndicate declined: "FDR's Other Scottish Terrier."

124 Roosevelt family friend: "December 1933—Franklin D. Roosevelt Day by Day," FDR Presidential Library, accessed August 31, 2021, http://www.fdrlibrary.marist.edu/daybyday/event/december-29-1933-2/.

124 laughter throughout the remarks: Glass, "FDR Defends Fala."

125 in December 1933: Elyse Wanshel, "FDR's German Shepherd, Major, Had a History of 'Biting Incidents,' Too," *HuffPost,* March 31, 2021, accessed May 31, 2021, https://www.huffpost.com/entry/major-fdr-biden-german-shepherd_n_6064b13cc5b6d5b7a695293a.

125 eggs *for eighteen people*: "Roosevelt Dog in Disgrace for Code Violation," *Pittsburgh Press,* February 27, 1934.

125 in Silver Spring, Maryland: "FDR's Dog, Winks," Presidential Pet Museum, January 23, 2016, accessed June 4, 2021, https://www.presidentialpetmuseum.com/pets/fdrs-dog-winks/.

125 espionage (that we know of): Charles B. MacDonald, *A Time for Trumpets: The Untold Story of the Battle of the Bulge* (New York: HarperCollins, 1997), 226.

126 "Do dogs really know": Jim Bishop, *FDR's Last Year: April 1944–April 1945* (New York: William Morrow, 1974), 590–91.

126 "until the master should return": Eleanor Roosevelt, *The Autobiography of Eleanor Roosevelt* (New York: Da Capo Press, 1992), 288.

126 his twelfth birthday: "Fala Biography."

127 "get a dog": Nadia Pflsum, "John Kasich Misquotes Truman on Dogs, Wins Ohio Anyway," Politifact, March 17, 2016, accessed June 5, 2021, https://www.politifact.com/factchecks/2016/mar/17/john-kasich/john-kasich-misquotes-truman-wins-ohio-anyway/.

128 a "dumb dog": Stanley Coren, *Why We Love the Dogs We Do: How to Find the Dog That Matches Your Personality* (New York: Simon & Schuster, 2002), ebook.

128 "the nation's property?": Coren, *Why We Love the Dogs.*

129 the local squirrels: Truman, *White House Pets.*

129 with President Truman: "All the Presidents' Squirrels Were Named Pete," Squirrels at the Door, February 15, 2016, accessed August 31, 2021, https://www.squirrelsatthedoor.com/2016/02/all-the-presidents-squirrels-were-named-pete/.

CHAPTER 7: COLD WAR DOGS

131 just over 3 million by 1960: Emily R. Kilby, "The Demographics of the U.S. Equine Population," Humane Society, September 16, 2021, https://www.humanesociety.org/sites/default/files/archive/assets/pdfs/hsp/soaiv_07_ch10.pdf.

133 openly loathed him: Robert A. Caro, *The Years of Lyndon Johnson: The Passage of Power* (New York: Knopf, 2012). Audiobook.

133 for the president's daughter: Caro, *The Years of Lyndon Johnson*.

133 the lesser-known Tex: Margaret Reed and Joan Lownds, *The Dogs of Camelot* (Latham, MD: Lyons Press, 2018). Audiobook.

134 of Iran's shah: Alex Q. Arbuckle, "Macaroni, The White House Pony Who Helped Inspire 'Sweet Caroline,'" Mashable, accessed July 22, 2021, https://mashable.com /feature/macaroni-the-white-house-pony.

134 around $50 billion annually: "Economic Impact of the United States Horse Industr," American Horse Council, September 16, 2021, https://www.horsecouncil .org/resources/economics/.

134 "our class lines": Lauren Vespoli, "How America Became Obsessed with Horses," *Smithsonian*, August 11, 2020, https://www.smithsonianmag.com/history /how-america-became-obsessed-horses-180975530/.

137 "for giving her to me": "White House Pets," Eisenhower Presidential Library, last modified June 6, 2019, accessed July 5, 2021, http://www.eisenhowerlibrary.gov /eisenhowers/white-house-pets.

138 his Gettysburg, Pennsylvania, farm: Kate Kelly, "The Eisenhower Dog, Heidi," America Comes Alive!, accessed July 6, 2021, https://americacomesalive.com/eisenhowers -weimeraner-heidi/.

138 peacefully on the farm: "President Dwight D. Eisenhower and His Dog, Heidi," White House Historical Association, accessed July 5, 2021, https://www.whitehousehistory .org/photos/president-dwight-d-eisenhower-and-his-dog-heidi.

139 before the election in 1960: Reed and Lownds, *Dogs of Camelot*.

141 "believe my mother had done that": Alison Gee, "Pushinka: A Cold War Puppy the Kennedys Loved," BBC News, January 6, 2014, accessed July 6, 2021, https://www.bbc .com/news/magazine-24837199.

141 devices and hidden bombs: Gee, "Pushinka."

142 "in your busy life": Oleg Yegorov, "Pushinka the Dog: How a Soviet Space Dog's Puppy Wound Up Living in the White House," Russia Beyond, April 19, 2018, accessed July 20, 2021, https://www.rbth.com/history/328099-pushinka-dog-space-dog-puppy-in -the-white-house.

142 canine playground exhibitions: Gee, "Pushinka."

143 part of Pushinka's temperament: Gee, "Pushinka."

143 "those damn Russians": C. David Heymann, *American Legacy: The Story of John and Caroline Kennedy* (New York: Atria Books, 2007). Audiobook.

143 "from nuclear destruction": Gee, "Pushinka."

144 "make some decisions": Reed and Lownds, *Dogs of Camelot.*

146 her husband's assassination: Reed and Lownds, *Dogs of Camelot.*

146 help hide her identity: Reed and Lownds, *Dogs of Camelot.*

146 replied simply, "Reporters": Reed and Lownds, *Dogs of Camelot.*

147 Kennedy family, particularly Clipper: Reed and Lownds, *Dogs of Camelot.*

151 "seemed to like it": Bud Boccone, "Pup Culture: 50 Years Later, LBJ's Still in the Doghouse," American Kennel Club, July 7, 2015, accessed July 6, 2021, https://www.akc.org/expert-advice/lifestyle/pup-culture-50-years-later-lbjs-still-in-the-doghouse.

151 "dignitaries at a state ball": "Him and Her," Presidential Pet Museum, July 22, 2013, accessed July 6, 2021, https://www.presidentialpetmuseum.com/pets/him-her.

151 White House grounds in 1966: "President Johnson's Dogs," LBJ Presidential Library, July 21, 2021, http://www.lbjlibrary.net/collections/quick-facts/lyndon-baines-johnson-dogs.html.

152 "best for the last": "LBJ: Dogs Have Always Been My Friends," YouTube, December 4, 2011, accessed July 7, 2021, https://youtu.be/BqdkeI5KwWI.

152 at the moon. Laughter ensues: "LBJ: Dogs Have Always Been My Friends."

153 "not your dog!": Traphes L. Bryant, *Dog Days at the White House: The Outrageous Memoirs of the Presidential Kennel Keeper* (New York: Ishi Press, 2010). Audiobook.

155 when LBJ left office: "President Johnson's Dogs."

155 ranch in 1969: "President Johnson's Dogs."

155 Museum of Modern Art in New York: Mo Rocca, *All the Presidents' Pets: The Inside Story of One Reporter Who Refused to Roll Over* (New York: Crown, 2004). Audiobook.

CHAPTER 8: DOGS OF THE SEVENTIES

157 euthanasia by 1985: Andrew N. Rowan and Tamara Kartal, "Dog Population and Dog Sheltering Trends in the United States of America," WBI Studies Repository, May 2018, accessed July 9, 2021, https://www.wellbeingintlstudiesrepository.org/demscapop/9/.

157 estimated 2.5 percent of pets: Zazie Todd, "America's Changing Relationship with the Pet Dog," *Companion Animal Psychology,* January 30, 2019, accessed July 9, 2021, https://www.companionanimalpsychology.com/2019/01/americas-changing -relationship-with-pet.html.

158 100 percent at present: Rowan and Kartal, "Dog Population and Dog Sheltering Trends."

158 pets as family members: Todd, "America's Changing Relationship with the Pet Dog."

159 sent to the Nixons: John Woestendiek, "The Dog Who Rescued Richard Nixon," *Baltimore Sun,* September 22, 2002, https://www.baltimoresun.com/entertainment/arts /bal-pets092202-story.html.

162 "we're gonna keep it": "Richard Nixon's Checkers Speech," History.com, accessed July 23, 2021, https://www.history.com/speeches/richard-nixons-checkers-speech.

163 Nixon referred to her as "he": Woestendiek, "The Dog Who Rescued Richard Nixon."

164 no less beloved: "Top Ten Breeds of the 1970s," American Kennel Club, last modified February 13, 2015, accessed July 5, 2021, https://www.akc.org/expert-advice/lifestyle /top-ten-breeds-of-the-1970s.

167 for the commander in chief: Walter R. Eletcher, "King Timahoe, an Irish Setter, Makes the White House His Domain," *New York Times,* January 11, 1973, https://www.nytimes .com/1973/01/11/archives/king-timahoe-an-irish-setter-makes-white-house-his-domain .html.

167 to receive treats: Kate Kelly, "The Dogs in the Nixon White House," America Comes Alive!, accessed July 9, 2021, https://americacomesalive.com/the-dogs-in-the-nixon -white-house.

168 would not have occurred: Kelly, "The Dogs in the Nixon White House."

168 collars for the event: Randee Dawn, "50 Years Ago, Tricia Nixon's White House Wedding Captivated the Nation," *Today,* June 11, 2021, accessed July 9, 2021, https://www.today.com/news/tricia-nixon-s-white-house-wedding-captivated-nation -50-years-t221157.

169 caught at least one: Kelly, "The Dogs in the Nixon White House."

171 to play with the puppy: Gerald Ford, *A Time to Heal: The Autobiography of Gerald R. Ford* (New York: Harper & Row, 1979). Audiobook.

173 "is seldom free": Gerald Ford, "Philadelphia, Pennsylvania: October 9, 1974," Gerald Ford Presidential Library, accessed July 8, 2021, https://www.fordlibrarymuseum.gov /library/document/0122/1252093.pdf.

174 could be fulfilled: "Liberty's Paw-tographs," Gerald Ford Presidential Library, accessed July 8, 2021, https://www.fordlibrarymuseum.gov/grf/pets3.asp.

174 for the comfort of the mother-to-be: "Gerald R. Ford Presidential Library and Museum: First Puppies," Tumblr, accessed July 9, 2021, https://fordlibrarymuseum.tumblr.com /post/129073219277/first-puppies-susan-ford-first-lady-betty-ford.

175 "get back to bed": Betty Ford, *The Times of My Life* (New York: Harper & Row, 1978). Audiobook.

175 through the process: "Gerald R. Ford Presidential Library: First Puppies."

177 Fords to various friends: "Gerald R. Ford Presidential Library: First Puppies."

177 members of the family: Roberto Manzotti, "The History of the Golden Retriever," Official Golden Retriever, accessed July 8, 2021, https://www.officialgoldenretriever .com/blog/dogs-world/history-golden-retriever.

179 Grits lived in: Kate Kelly, "The Carter Family and Amy's Dog, Grits." America Comes Alive!, accessed July 5, 2021. https://americacomesalive.com/carter-family-dog-grits/.

179 tree on the property: Donnie Radcliffe, "Amy Carter's Shady White House Hideaway," *Washington Post,* March 18, 1977, accessed August 22, 2021, https://www .washingtonpost.com/archive/lifestyle/1977/03/18/amy-carters-shady-white-house -hideaway/afe7a737-0870-45c5-87d4-a82f1b17a48b/.

179 since their days in Georgia: "Grits in the Doghouse," *New York Times,* September 12, 1979. Clipping sent to the author by the Jimmy Carter Presidential Library in Atlanta, Georgia.

180 for the test: Truman, *White House Pets.*

180 "was through with Grits!": "First Ladies' Press Secretaries," C-SPAN, July 6, 2004, accessed July 7, 2021, https://www.c-span.org/video/?181646-1/ladies-press-secretaries.

180 gearing up for reelection: Jim O'Grady, "How Jimmy Carter's Face-Off with a Rabbit Changed the Presidency," WNYC, February 17, 2014, accessed July 23, 2021, https:// www.wnyc.org/story/hare-brained-history-curious-case-jimmy-carter-v-rabbit.

180 "was not White House broken": "People, September 24, 1979," *Time,* accessed August 22, 2021, http://content.time.com/time/magazine/article/0,9171,947422,00.html.

183 *32 million cat-owning households:* "U.S. Pet Ownership Statistics," American Veterinary Medical Association, accessed August 6, 2021, https://www.avma.org/resources-tools /reports-statistics/us-pet-ownership-statistics.

183 *cats-per-household ratio:* Roberto A. Ferdman and Christopher Ingraham, "Where Cats Are More Popular Than Dogs in the U.S.—and All Over the World," *Washington Post,* July 28, 2014, https://www.washingtonpost.com/news/wonk/wp/2014/07/28/where -cats-are-more-popular-than-dogs-in-the-u-s-and-all-over-the-world/.

184 *almost 90 million dogs:* Rowan and Kartal, "Dog Population and Dog Sheltering Trends in the United States of America."

184 *three-to-one advantage:* Ferdman and Ingraham, "Where Cats Are More Popular Than Dogs."

184 *more likely to own dogs:* Ferdman and Ingraham, "Where Cats Are More Popular Than Dogs."

184 *American Pet Products Association:* Rowan and Kartal, "Dog Population and Dog Sheltering Trends in the United States of America."

186 *"no good pictures":* "First Ladies' Press Secretaries."

187 *poster child Kristen Ellis:* "Presidential Pets," Ronald Reagan Presidential Library, accessed July 31, 2021, https://www.reaganlibrary.gov/reagans/reagan-administration /presidential-pets.

187 *be gifted is unknown:* "Kristen Nicole Ellis Memorial Page." Middendorf-Bullock Funeral Home, 2017, accessed August 9, 2021, https://www.middendorfbullock.com /obituary/Kristen-Ellis.

187 *"going to grow this big":* "First Ladies' Press Secretaries."

187 *Edith Luckett Davis:* "Presidential Pets," Ronald Reagan Presidential Library.

189 *"an unauthorized leak":* "First Ladies' Press Secretaries."

190 *Thanksgiving holiday of 1985:* "Presidential Pets," Ronald Reagan Presidential Library.

190 *Park in Williamsburg, Virginia:* "Ronald Reagan's Dog Lucky," Presidential Pet Museum, July 21, 2013, accessed July 31, 2021, https://www.presidentialpetmuseum .com/pets/lucky/.

191 *to Los Angeles in 1989:* "Presidential Pets," Ronald Reagan Presidential Library.

192 than his own memoir: "Washington Journal: Presidential Dogs," C-SPAN, August 25, 1997, accessed July 30, 2021, https://www.c-span.org/video/?89833-1/presidential -dogs.

193 asking for a puppy: AP Archives, "President George H.W. Bush and His Wife Barbara Show Off First Dog Millie's New Puppies," YouTube, 2016, accessed July 30, 2021, https://youtu.be/bOpOvIYsFsI.

193 "every week or so": Associated Press, "Millie, 'First Dog' in the Bush White House, Dies at Age 12," *Los Angeles Times,* May 21, 1997, accessed August 1, 2021, https://www .latimes.com/archives/la-xpm-1997-05-21-mn-60931-story.html.

193 "homely springer spaniel": Andrew Beaujon, "Washingtonian Once Called George H.W. Bush's Dog Ugly, and I'm Here to Correct the Record," *Washingtonian,* December 3, 2018, accessed July 30, 2021, https://www.washingtonian.com/2018/12/03/ washingtonian-once-called-george-h-w-bushs-dog-ugly-and-im-here-to-correct-the -record/.

193 "the dog biscuits": Beaujon, "Washingtonian Once Called George H.W. Bush's Dog Ugly."

194 an episode of *The Simpsons*: Robb Fritz, "History's a Bitch: A Dog Walk Through Time— Millie's Book," *McSweeney's,* May 16, 2012, accessed July 31, 2021, https://www .mcsweeneys.net/articles/millies-book.

195 at an alarming rate: Ilona Baliūnaitć and James Caunt, "George Bush Sr. Once Wrote This Funny Memo to the White House Staff Regarding His Fat Dog Ranger," Bored Panda, 2020, July 31, 2021, https://www.boredpanda.com/george-bush-sr-fat-dog-memo/.

196 her literacy foundation: Fritz, "History's a Bitch."

196 first year of publication: AP News, "Royalties from 'Millie's Book' Top $1 Million," July 10, 1991, accessed August 8, 2021, https://apnews.com/article /e3ea5499dbcaee0396cf8768c96f112c.

196 "the dog mess with you": "First Ladies' Press Secretaries."

196 "than those two bozos": Fritz, "History's a Bitch."

196 pneumonia at age twelve: Fritz, "History's a Bitch."

198 of her music teacher: "About Socks and Buddy," The White House, Spring 1999, accessed July 27, 2021, https://clintonwhitehouse4.archives.gov/WH/kids/inside/html /Spring99-4.html.

198 after the 1992 election: Chloe Bryan, "Remember When House Republicans Went After Socks the Cat?" Mashable, June 4, 2017, accessed July 26, 2021, https://mashable.com/article/socks-the-cat-gop-investigation.

199 not to do so again: Reuters, "The Transition: Hands Off Cat, Clinton Warns," *New York Times,* November 19, 1992, https://www.nytimes.com/1992/11/19/us/the-transition-hands-off-cat-clinton-warns.html.

199 by Kermit the Frog: "Socks the Cat," Muppet Wiki, accessed July 27, 2021, https://muppet.fandom.com/wiki/Socks_the_Cat.

199 *Socks the Cat Rocks the Hill:* Scott Meslow, "Today, Let Us Remember the Bizarre-Ass Video Game about Hillary Clinton's Cat," *GQ,* November 8, 2016, accessed July 27, 2021, https://www.gq.com/story/hillary-clinton-socks-the-cat-video-game.

199 kids' White House website: Bryan, "Remember When House Republicans Went After Socks."

199 First Feline fan mail: Bryan, "Remember When House Republicans Went After Socks."

199 in Federalsburg, Maryland: "Statement: A Tribute to Buddy," Clinton Foundation, December 11, 2003, accessed July 28, 2021, https://www.clintonfoundation.org/press-and-news/general/statement-a-tribute-to-buddy/.

199 for five decades: "Statement: A Tribute to Buddy."

200 "taken to separate quarters": "First Ladies' Press Secretaries."

200 make peace between his two animals: "President Clinton Touts Economy While President-elect Bush Warns of Slowdown," CNN.com, January 12, 2001, accessed July 29, 2021, http://edition.cnn.com/TRANSCRIPTS/0101/12/ip.00.html.

200 hissing at Buddy: "As Peace Process Fails, First Cat Prepares for Exile," *New York Times,* January 10, 2001, https://www.nytimes.com/2001/01/10/us/as-peace-process-fails-first-cat-prepares-for-exile.html.

200 the National Park Foundation: Bryan, "Remember When House Republicans Went After Socks."

201 time in the White House: Sharon Cotliar, "The Clintons Bid Farewell to Socks the Cat," *People,* February 20, 2009, accessed July 25, 2021, https://people.com/celebrity/the-clintons-bid-farewell-to-socks-the-cat/.

201 scene could retrieve him: "Former First Dog Buddy Killed by Car," CNN.com, January 3, 2002, accessed July 26, 2021, https://www.cnn.com/2002/US/01/03/buddy.killed/index.html.

201 close to twenty years old: Cotliar, "The Clintons Bid Farewell to Socks."

CHAPTER 10: NEW MILLENNIUM DOGS

204 would get sick and die: Benj Edwards, "The Golden Age of Virtual Pets," PCMag.com, April 10, 2018, accessed July 29, 2021, https://www.pcmag.com/news/the-golden-age-of-virtual-pets.

204 users' pet monsters: Edwards, "The Golden Age of Virtual Pets."

204 exercise via a built-in pedometer: Edwards, "The Golden Age of Virtual Pets."

204 a Brink's armored truck: Joseph Pereira, "Retailers Bet Virtual Pets Will Be the Next Big Craze," *Wall Street Journal,* May 2, 1997, https://www.wsj.com/articles/SB862538645580947500.

204 prices as low as $9.99: Pereira, "Retailers Bet Virtual Pets."

205 a distraction—banned the toys: Debra Barayuga, "Electronic Pets Peep Their Last at Isle Schools," *Honolulu Star-Bulletin,* June 2, 1997, http://archives.starbulletin.com/97/06/02/news/story2.html.

205 to retrieve the beeping gizmo: Pereira, "Retailers Bet Virtual Pets."

205 could be reset after a pet's death: "A Special Place for Tamagotchi Interment," CNN, January 18, 1998, accessed July 30, 2021, http://edition.cnn.com/WORLD/9801/18/tamagotchi/.

205 with the player/owner decreased: "Nintendogs," Nintendogs Wiki, accessed August 6, 2021, https://nintendogs.fandom.com/wiki/Nintendogs.

206 part of the game's launch: Spencer Rutledge, "The Sims 4 Partners with SPCA in Celebrating Pets Everywhere," Hardcore Gamer, November 13, 2017, August 8, 2021, https://hardcoregamer.com/news/the-sims-4-partners-with-spca-in-celebrating-pets-everywhere/279256/.

208 his wife, Laura, in 2000: "Barney & Miss Beazley," George W. Bush Presidential Library and Museum, accessed August 14, 2021, https://www.georgewbushlibrary.smu.edu/Home/The-President-and-Family/The-Bush-Family/Barney-and-Miss-Beazley-Biography.aspx.

209 "[to the communications team]": Jimmy Orr, "R.I.P., Barney: How 'Barney Cam' Made George W. Bush's Dog a Web Star," *Los Angeles Times,* February 6, 2013, https://www.latimes.com/nation/la-na-barney-cam-20130206-story.html.

210 "That is *awesome*": Jimmy Orr interview with the author on June 4, 2021.

210 *how do we do this*: Orr interview.

210 lighting for the president: Elisabeth Bumiller, "Barney Cam Is 'Reloaded' for a Christmas Sequel from the White House," *New York Times,* December 13, 2003, https://www.nytimes.com/2003/12/13/us/barney-cam-is-reloaded-for-a-christmas-sequel-from-the-white-house.html.

210 to live without one: Orr, "R.I.P., Barney."

210 was torturing the terrier: Orr, "R.I.P., Barney."

210 "the son I never had": Bumiller, "Barney Cam Is 'Reloaded.'"

210 dog's-eye view of the decorations: Orr, "R.I.P., Barney."

211 couldn't believe it, either: Orr interview.

211 on the White House website: Bumiller, "Barney Cam Is 'Reloaded.'"

211 "which had no plot": Bumiller, "Barney Cam Is 'Reloaded.'"

211 "just not going to work": David Almacy interview with the author on August 8, 2021.

213 "We're good": Almacy interview.

213 "didn't like strangers": Eun Kyung Kim, "Jenna Bush Hager: Former First Dog Barney 'Was a Real Jerk,'" *Today,* December 5, 2013, accessed May 15, 2021, https://www.today.com/pets/jenna-bush-hager-former-first-dog-barney-was-real-jerk-2d11697960.

213 "and separated them": Almacy interview.

214 "done with the paparazzi": Associated Press, "President Bush's Dog Bites Reporter: Is That News?" *Los Angeles Times,* November 7, 2008, https://www.latimes.com/la-on-dogbite7-2008nov07-story.html.

214 "we have with our pets": Almacy interview.

214 "just thinking about it": Almacy interview.

215 often seem to enjoy the work: Linda Lombardi, "Therapy Dogs Work Miracles. But Do They Like Their Jobs?" *National Geographic,* May 1, 2018, https://www.nationalgeographic.com/animals/article/animals-dogs-therapy-health-pets.

215 "a joyous, uplifting moment": Ari Fleischer interview with the author on May 3, 2021.

215 a part owner of the team: Deborah Orin, "White House Dynasty?—It's Just a Matter of Pet-igree," *New York Post,* July 1, 1999, https://nypost.com/1999/07/01/white-house -dynasty-its-just-a-matter-of-pet-igree/.

215 "a grudge against him": Eyder Peralta, "Miss Beazley, Former First Dog, Keeper of Bush Cats," NPR, May 17, 2014, accessed August 14, 2021, https://www.npr.org/sections /thetwo-way/2014/05/17/313449742/miss-beazley-former-first-dog-keeper-of-bush-cats -dies.

216 "is coming with us!": "Bo and Sunny," Obama Foundation, accessed August 12, 2021, www.Obama.org/gallery/bo-Sunny.

217 suffered from allergies: Stacy St. Clair, "Allergist Offers Advice on Obama Dog Debate," *Chicago Tribune,* November 11, 2008, https://www.chicagotribune.com/news /chi-first-puppynov11-story.html.

217 reactions in allergy sufferers: St. Clair, "Allergist Offers Advice."

219 "better than most senators": Jesse Lee, "Senator Kennedy and Bo," Obama White House Archives, August 28, 2009, accessed August 13, 2021, https://obamawhitehouse .archives.gov/blog/2009/08/28/senator-kennedy-bo.

219 "turn it on in public": Dana Lewis, interview with the author on April 19, 2021.

220 headed out for more goodies: Lewis interview.

220 "has a right to expect": Barack Obama, *A Promised Land* (New York: Crown, 2020). Audiobook.

220 and children's hospitals: Lewis interview.

221 Children's National Medical Center: Alicia M. Cohn, "Michelle Obama Takes Bo to Visit Children's Hospital," *The Hill,* December 14, 2012, accessed August 12, 2021, https:// thehill.com/blogs/blog-briefing-room/news/273057-michelle-obama-takes-bo-to-visit -childrens-hospital.

221 Walter Reed National Military Medical Center: Todd Veazie, "First Lady Visits Military Families at Walter Reed National Military Medical Center," Obama White House Archives, March 22, 2013, accessed August 12, 2021, https://obamawhitehouse .archives.gov/blog/2013/03/22/first-lady-michelle-obama-visits-military-families-fisher -house-and-walter-reed-nati.

222 children and veterans was, she says, "priceless": Lewis interview.

222 Yosses recalled, was a "doggie success": Bill Yosses, email interview with the author on April 21, 2021.

222 managed to dislodge them: Lewis interview.

222 "the perfect little sister for Bo": Linda Feldmann, "New Little Girl Arrives at White House. Meet Sunny Obama," *Christian Science Monitor,* August 20, 2013, accessed September 15, 2021, https://www.csmonitor.com/USA/Politics/Decoder/2013/0820 /New-little-girl-arrives-at-White-House.-Meet-Sunny-Obama.

222 Kidnap either Bo or Sunny: Emily Jane Fox, "The Secret Service Just Thwarted a Plot to Kidnap Obama's Dogs," *Vanity Fair,* January 8, 2016, https://www.vanityfair.com /news/2016/01/secret-service-thwarted-plot-to-kidnap-obamas-dogs.

223 once bit a White House guest: Liz Eustachewich, "Sunny Obama Bit a White House Guest's Face." *New York Post,* January 12, 2017, https://nypost.com/2017/01/12/sunny -obama-bit-a-white-house-guests-face/.

223 for quite some time: Lindsay Kimble, "POTUS Pet Peeve: Sunny the Dog Likes Doing Her Business Right Outside His Office—'I Have to Run Out and Catch Her!'" *People,* December 9, 2016. https://people.com/politics/obamas-dog-sunny-poops -in-the-white-house/.

223 "had great hair": Michael Levenson, "Bo, the Obamas' Portuguese Water Dog, Dies," *New York Times,* May 8, 2021, https://www.nytimes.com/2021/05/08/us/politics /obama-dog-bo-dead.html.

CHAPTER 11: RESCUE ERA DOGS

225 the no-kill Delaware Humane Association: Joan Page McKenna, "Major Is Delaware's First Shelter Dog in the White House," *Delaware Today,* January 4, 2021, accessed August 19, 2021, https://delawaretoday.com/life-style/major-biden-shelter-dog-white -house/.

225 "as a presidential companion": Jane Velez-Mitchell interview with the author on August 18, 2021.

226 of the COVID-19 pandemic: Megan McCluskey, "Rescue Animals Are TIME's 2020 Pet of the Year," *Time,* December 9, 2020, https://time.com/5912616/pet-of-the-year -2020-rescue-animals/.

226 strays or shelter animals: "Pet Statistics," ASPCA, accessed August 21, 2021, https:// www.aspca.org/helping-people-pets/shelter-intake-and-surrender/pet-statistics.

226 four dogs are purebred: "Adopting from an Animal Shelter or Rescue Group," Humane Society of the United States, August 21, 2021, https://www.humanesociety.org/resources/adopting-animal-shelter-or-rescue-group.

226 not behavioral difficulties: "Adopting from an Animal Shelter or Rescue Group."

226 "bred in puppy mills and sold": Velez-Mitchell interview.

227 shelter are not adopted: "Adopting from an Animal Shelter or Rescue Group."

227 returned to their homes: "Pet Statistics," ASPCA.

227 claimed before being euthanized, Karen Johnson interview with the author on August 3, 2021.

227 deaths a year: "Pet Statistics," ASPCA.

227 "a hedge against loneliness": McCluskey, "Rescue Animals Are TIME's 2020 Pet of the Year."

228 microchipping common with rescues: "Top Reasons to Adopt a Pet." Humane Society of the United States, accessed September 16, 2021. https://www.humanesociety.org/resources/top-reasons-adopt-pet.

228 "might not have thought of": Jeremy Bernard interview with the author on September 3, 2021.

229 would feel "phony": Antonia Noori Farzan, "Trump, the First President in a Century with No Dog, Explains Why: 'I Don't Have Any Time,'" *Washington Post,* February 12, 2019, https://www.washingtonpost.com/nation/2019/02/12/trump-first-president-century-with-no-dog-explains-why-i-dont-have-any-time/.

230 "ultimate fighter, ultimate everything": Brittany Shammas, "Trump Honors Conan, the Military Dog Injured in the Baghdadi Raid," *Washington Post,* November 25, 2019, https://www.washingtonpost.com/politics/2019/11/25/trump-honors-conan-military-dog-injured-baghdadi-raid/.

230 she "appeared to decline": Shammas, "Trump Honors Conan."

230 scratch behind the ears: Shammas, "Trump Honors Conan."

231 the VP's daughter Charlotte: Elizabeth S. Mitchell, "The Truth About Mike Pence's Pet Bunny," The List, October 28, 2020, accessed August 19, 2020, https://www.thelist.com/268125/the-truth-about-mike-pences-pet-bunny/.

231 A21 (an organization combating human trafficking): Associated Press, "Sales Multiply for Pence and Oliver Rabbit Books," *Chicago Tribune,* March 26, 2018, https://www.chicagotribune.com/entertainment/books/ct-sales-pence-oliver-rabbit -books-20180326-story.html.

231 official Bundo Instagram account: Associated Press, "Sales Multiply."

232 the family in June of 2017: Karin Brulliard, "An Important Update on the Pets of the Executive Branch," *Washington Post,* June 20, 2017, https://www.washingtonpost.com /news/animalia/wp/2017/06/20/an-important-update-on-the-pets-of-the-executive -branch/?outputType=amp.

232 "so I named him Harley": Holly V. Hays, "Here's Why Vice President Pence Named His Puppy Harley," *USA Today,* June 20, 2017, accessed August 25, 2021, https://www .usatoday.com/story/news/politics/onpolitics/2017/06/20/vice-president-pence-named -his-new-dog-harley/413891001/.

232 "shouldn't Harley be DOTUS?": Brulliard, "An Important Update."

233 "the Pences are yokels": McKay Copins, "God's Plan for Mike Pence," *The Atlantic,* January/February 2018, https://www.theatlantic.com/magazine /archive/2018/01/gods-plan-for-mike-pence/546569/.

233 had ever said this: Arturo Garcia, "Did Donald Trump Say It Was 'Low Class' for Mike Pence to Bring Pets to Washington?" *Snopes,* January 2, 2018, accessed August 25, 2021, https://www.snopes.com/fact-check/did-trump-say-low-class-pets/.

234 a photo of the Biden dogs: Jeff Beer, "New Biden Ad Plays Presidential Dog Card After Trump's Rabid Debate," *Fast Company,* September 30, 2020, accessed August 18, 2021, https://www.fastcompany.com/90558659/new-biden-ad-plays-the-presidential-dog -card-after-trumps-rabid-debate.

236 the Delaware Humane Association: Laura Entis, "Major Biden's 'Indoguration' Raises $202K for Delaware Humane Association," *PR Week,* February 11, 2021, accessed August 20, 2021, https://www.prweek.com/article/1707071/major-bidens-indoguration -raises-202k-delaware-humane-association.

236 indicating the dogs: Alexandra Jaffe, "Biden Dogs to Make Appearance During Puppy Bowl," ABC News, February 5, 2021, accessed August 20, 2021, https://abcnews .go.com/Sports/wireStory/biden-dogs-make-appearance-puppy-bowl-75708505.

237 was not particularly serious: "Joe Biden Fractures Foot After Slipping While Playing with Dog," *Guardian,* November 29, 2020, accessed August 22, 2021, https://www.theguardian.com/us-news/2020/nov/29/joe-biden-twists-his-ankle-after-slipping-while-playing-with-dog.

237 for additional training: Kate Bennett, "Major Biden to Get Training After Two Biting Incidents," CNN, April 12, 2021, accessed August 20, 2021, https://www.cnn.com/2021/04/12/politics/major-biden-training/index.html.

237 upon recovering from the assault: Rachel Brodsky, "Martin Short Joins SNL as Second Gentleman Doug Emhoff, Gets 'Mauled' by Biden's Dog Major," *Independent,* March 28, 2021, accessed August 20, 2021, https://www.independent.co.uk/arts-entertainment/tv/news/martin-short-snl-doug-emhoff-b1823484.html.

238 all injuries were minor: Dareh Gregorian and Lauren Egan, "'Minor' Major Issues: Emails Show Biden Dog Was Nippier Than White House said," NBC News, August 27, 2021, accessed August 31, 2021, https://www.nbcnews.com/news/animal-news/minor-major-issues-emails-show-biden-dog-was-nippier-white-n1277814.

238 to the White House: Gregorian and Egan, "'Minor' Major Issues."

238 just about anywhere: Justin Gomez and Morgan Winsor, "Biden's German Shepherd Major Back in Doghouse After Another Biting Incident," ABC News, March 31, 2021, accessed April 19, 2021, https://abcnews.go.com/Politics/bidens-german-shepherd-major-back-doghouse-biting-incident/story?id=76784280.

238 South Lawn with his dogs: Margaret Hartmann, "President Biden's Weirdest White House Habits," *Intelligencer,* August 14, 2021, accessed August 25, 2021, https://nymag.com/intelligencer/article/president-bidens-weirdest-white-house-habits.html.

238 is actually a Republican: Sharon Coolidge, "'You've Got a Great Dog There, Kid.' Wonder the Dog Slightly Injured at Biden Town Hall. She's Survived Worse," *Cincinnati Enquirer,* July 23, 2021, https://www.cincinnati.com/story/news/2021/07/23/biden-town-hall-who-dog-wonder/8062291002/.

239 during the exchange: Coolidge, "'You've Got a Great Dog There, Kid.'"

239 "but absolutely critical": Shannon Keith interview with the author on August 25, 2021.

241 new biting or aggression incidents: Michael LaRosa email to the author, December 21, 2021.

241 "to live for humans and animals": Jane Velez-Mitchell email to the author, December 21, 2021.

241 James and James's wife, Sara: Velez-Mitchell email.

241 photos of his new dog: Alexandra Jaffe, "Biden, First Lady Visit Hospitalized Kids on Christmas Eve," AP News, December 24, 2021, accessed January 10, 2022, https://apnews.com/article/joe-biden-lifestyle-jill-biden-holidays.

241 around the globe for their service: "Commander, the Newest Member of President Joe Biden and First Lady Jill Biden's Family," *USA Today*, Dec. 28, 2021, accessed January 10, 2022, https://www.usatoday.com/picture-gallery/news/politics/2021/12/28/meet -commander-presidential-puppy/9030197002/.

241 with the vice president's grandchildren: Elena Moore, "President Biden's Dog Champ Dies," NPR, June 19, 2021, accessed August 20, 2021, https://www.npr.org/2021/06/19/1008356025/champ-joe-biden-dog-dies-white -house-german-shepherd.

241 in need of a bath: Ryan Parker, "Newsmax Host and Guests Skewered After Mocking President Biden's Senior Dog, Champ," *Hollywood Reporter,* February 20, 2021, accessed August 20, 2021, https://www.hollywoodreporter.com/news/politics-news /newsmax-host-and-guests-skewered-after-mocking-president-bidens-senior-dog -champ-4135898/.

241 "miss him always": Elena Moore, "President Biden's Dog Champ Dies," NPR, June 19, 2021, accessed August 20, 2021, https://www.npr.org/2021/06/19/1008356025/champ -joe-biden-dog-dies-white-house-german-shepherd.

241 "waiting in the wings": Hartmann, "President Biden's Weirdest White House Habits."

241 delayed the cat's arrival: Katie Rogers, "Jill Biden Is Chasing the President's Most Elusive Campaign Promise: Unity," *New York Times,* September 19, 2021, https://www .nytimes.com/2021/09/19/us/politics/jill-biden.html?referringSource=articleShare.

ABOUT THE AUTHOR

Andrew Hager serves as historian-in-residence for the Presidential Pet Museum, a position he has held since 2017. Prior to that, he taught middle school social studies and language arts for a decade. Andrew is legally blind and travels with a black Labrador retriever named Sammy. He lives with his wife, Kristy, and their two children, Mia and Ian, in the suburbs outside of Baltimore, Maryland. In addition to Sammy, the family has a fluffy mixed-breed rescue named Emmy and two cats, Sophia and Olivia.